D1391898

The
Mercury
Retrograde
Book

The
Mercury
Retrograde
Book

Turn chaos into creativity to repair, renew and revamp your life

YASMIN BOLAND
& KIM FARNELL

HAY HOUSE

Carlsbad, California • New York City
London • Sydney • New Delhi

Published in the United Kingdom by:
Hay House UK Ltd, The Sixth Floor, Watson House,
54 Baker Street, London W1U 7BU
Tel: +44 (0)20 3927 7290; Fax: +44 (0)20 3927 7291
www.hayhouse.co.uk

Published in the United States of America by:
Hay House Inc., PO Box 5100, Carlsbad, CA 92018-5100
Tel: (1) 760 431 7695 or (800) 654 5126
Fax: (1) 760 431 6948 or (800) 650 5115; www.hayhouse.com

Published in Australia by:
Hay House Australia Ltd, 18/36 Ralph St, Alexandria NSW 2015
Tel: (61) 2 9669 4299; Fax: (61) 2 9669 4144; www.hayhouse.com.au

Published in India by:
Hay House Publishers India, Muskaan Complex,
Plot No.3, B-2, Vasant Kunj, New Delhi 110 070
Tel: (91) 11 4176 1620; Fax: (91) 11 4176 1630; www.hayhouse.co.in

Text © Yasmin Boland, 2019

The moral rights of the author have been asserted.

All rights reserved. No part of this book may be reproduced by any
mechanical, photographic or electronic process, or in the form of a
phonographic recording; nor may it be stored in a retrieval system,
transmitted or otherwise be copied for public or private use, other
than for 'fair use' as brief quotations embodied in articles and reviews,
without prior written permission of the publisher.

The information given in this book should not be treated as a substitute
for professional medical advice; always consult a medical practitioner.
Any use of information in this book is at the reader's discretion and
risk. Neither the author nor the publisher can be held responsible for
any loss, claim or damage arising out of the use, or misuse, of the
suggestions made, the failure to take medical advice or for any material
on third-party websites.

A catalogue record for this book is available from the British Library.

Hardcover ISBN: 978-1-78817-354-4
Audiobook ISBN: 978-1-78817-382-7
E-book ISBN: 978-1-78817-356-8

Printed and bound by CPI Group (UK) Ltd, Croydon, CR0 4YY

Contents

Authors' Note

This book is truly a collaborative effort. It started life as an e-book which we co-wrote and Yasmin designed and offered for sale on her website. The Hay House UK team spotted it there and asked for several new sections to be added and for existing content to be tweaked, and from there it evolved into the book you're holding now.

Mercury retrograde is a phenomenon that even many non-astrologers have heard of. We think it's more than worth learning about, and that by reading this book you'll discover how to make it work to your advantage.

We hope you love the book!

Yasmin and Kim

Introduction

Mercury Retrograde – Myth or Fact?

This book is all about the retrograde cycle of the planet Mercury. So, let's first define Mercury...

Mercury is the communications planet. Whenever you open your mouth to talk, or when you write something – anything from an e-mail to a novel or beyond – or even if you just think or listen to someone, you're using your Mercury. It's the mind planet and it guides how you talk, write, otherwise express yourself and take in information. It's your intellectual process. Knowing which sign and House Mercury is in will tell you how you think and express yourself, and even how you negotiate.

Mercury is also the transport planet and the planet of short journeys and commuting. It governs trade and commerce. Plus, it governs your wit, thoughts and thirst for knowledge and your desire and ability to learn. Do you think quickly? Do you like to analyse things? Are you a fast learner? Can you keep secrets? These sorts of questions will be answered when you learn about your Mercury.

Mercury is the trickster and it's also the quicksilver planet. If someone is a fast talker or a smooth talker, it's thanks to their Mercury. If they think too hard, or overthink, or can't make decisions, look to their Mercury for an explanation.

What causes a planetary retrograde?

These days, with the rising interest in astrology, more and more people, even non-astrologers, seem to have heard about Mercury retrograde – when Mercury appears to move backwards in the sky. That said, there are also many misunderstandings surrounding Mercury retrograde – mostly that it's all doom and gloom or somehow bad luck, which it's not. This is why we wrote this book: to dispel the myths and help you get the most of this planetary phenomenon which has a potentially positive side to it.

Obviously, planets don't actually turn around and start moving backwards, even though, from our viewpoint on Earth, it sometimes appears as if they do. It's all an optical illusion, due to the relative positions of the planet and Earth and how they move around the Sun.

Mercury is the closest planet to the Sun and its orbit is shorter than Earth's – a mere 88 days compared to our 365 days, which means that Mercury experiences four years in the time it takes us to complete one orbit of the Sun. Mercury's shorter orbit creates an optical illusion in that it appears to speed past Earth, slow down and then move in a backwards loop, giving us Mercury retrograde. It's the planetary equivalent of runners on a race track: the inner track is shorter than the outer track.

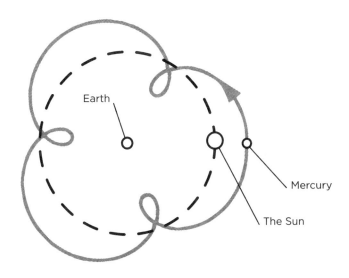

A graphic representation of the orbit of Mercury around the Sun, from our point of view here on Earth. The 'loops' show when Mercury is in apparent retrograde motion.

This is how planetary retrogrades work from our vantage point. The Earth 'sees' Mercury ahead, but the Earth moves faster than Mercury so as we catch up and then overtake it, Mercury appears to go backwards in the sky. This means that instead of progressing forwards through the zodiac, from one sign to another, Mercury appears to 'reverse' through whatever sign it was in when the retrograde started. It's an illusion, but a meaningful one, symbolically.

Mercury isn't the only planet that goes retrograde – they all do (with the exception of the Sun and Moon, which aren't planets). When a planet goes retrograde, we get a stalling in the proceedings connected to that planet. Mercury retrograde is the best known of all the planetary retrogrades though, and it happens three or four times a year or about 20 per cent of the time.

Whether it's moving forwards or backwards, Mercury in the skies triggers Mercury issues as it goes. Because Mercury is the trickster, when it goes retrograde its influence works differently – its energy intensifies and things seem to go awry. However, as you'll discover, you can work consciously with Mercury's energies when it's retrograde and use them very much to your advantage.

Common myths about Mercury retrograde

Before we move on to exploring how to maximize Mercury's energies, let's start by dispelling a few common myths about Mercury retrograde. We've already explained why Mercury appearing to go backwards is an illusion, and another common myth is that we can't see Mercury in the sky when it's retrograde because it's too close to the Sun.

The truth is that Mercury is usually too close to the Sun to be seen. But when Mercury is about to go retrograde, it's far away enough from the Sun to be visible to the naked eye. Just as Mercury's turning retrograde, we can briefly see it as a faint light after sunset, close to where the Sun has just set. At the end of its retrograde phase, we can see it just before sunrise.

Many people also buy into the myth that 'all these things going wrong in my life are due to Mercury being retrograde' or believe 'it causes nothing but problems'. But if you tend to miscommunicate, mess up your travel plans, miss appointments, lose things and delete important emails, you'll carry on doing this whether Mercury is retrograde or not – it's not Mercury's fault. The truth is things do go wrong under Mercury retrograde – and particularly with communications – all of which are inconvenient, annoying and frustrating. In this book, however, you'll not only learn how you can prepare to avoid the worst effects of Mercury retrograde, but also how to use it to your advantage – for example, it's a great time to deal with what you've left unresolved in the past or make plans for the future.

Shadow phases

The periods just before Mercury goes retrograde and just after it goes 'direct' again (in other words, the retrograde cycle ends), are known as the shadow phases. During these times you might feel the effects of Mercury retrograde even more; this is because the start and finish of any cycle in astrology is always the strongest.

The **pre-shadow phase** – before Mercury goes retrograde – gives you the chance to prepare for its effects. This isn't an ideal time to make decisions and it's a good idea to be as flexible as you can. The **post-shadow phase** (sometimes called the 'echo') – after the retrograde – allows you to process its effects. It's a good idea to tread cautiously and wait before putting new plans into action.

These shadow phases mean that the effects of Mercury retrograde go on for much longer than the time it's actually retrograde. The most frustrating time is often when Mercury is about to turn retrograde or direct – when it 'stations'. This is a period of stillness and reflection, so it's not the best time to make plans.

Working out the shadow phase

The shadow phases last about two weeks before and two weeks after Mercury retrograde. If you're just starting out in astrology, you really just need to pay attention to the start and finish dates of the Mercury retrograde cycles (*see Appendix, pages 179–182*). However, if you're (or become) more advanced in your studies, and start working with degrees of the zodiac, here's how the shadow phases work:

▶ While still moving forwards, Mercury moves over the degree on which it will eventually end its retrograde – let's call it degree X. This marks the start of the first shadow phase.

▶ Mercury keeps moving forwards through the first shadow phase and eventually stations on a later degree – let's call this degree Y, which is also known as Mercury Retrograde Station – and starts to go retrograde. This marks the end of the first shadow phase and the start of the 'regular' retrograde cycle.

▶ Mercury goes as far back in the zodiac that it's going to go for this cycle – back to degree X, which is also known as Mercury Direct Station. This marks the end of the retrograde cycle and the start of the second shadow phase.

▶ Mercury then moves forwards again, re-covering the part of the zodiac that it just retrograded over. This is the second shadow phase of this cycle. Eventually Mercury reaches degree Y (where it initially went retrograde), ending the second shadow phase.

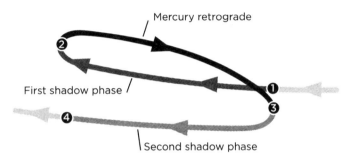

Mercury's shadow phases

1. Degree X marks the start of the first shadow phase.

2. Degree Y, or Mercury Retrograde Station, marks the end of the first shadow phase and the start of the retrograde cycle.

3. Mercury stations back at degree X, also known as Mercury Direct Station, marking the end of the retrograde cycle and the start of the second shadow phase.

4. Mercury moves forwards through second shadow phase before reaching degree Y, marking the end the second shadow phase.

Common effects of the retrograde

When a planet goes retrograde, the things associated with it slow down and unresolved or unfinished business is often the result. We can also get indications that things are happening behind the scenes and it's time to review the affairs of that planet. For Mercury retrograde, that means paying especially close attention to communication, transport and new technology. Mercury also rules buying and selling, contracts and agreements, and important documents.

That's why you might feel as if you have everything figured out and then Mercury goes into retrograde and makes you feel as if the world has gone mad: the best-laid plans don't go anywhere and you start to drift off mid-sentence. You may also find:

◗ Gadgets that were in perfect working order suddenly break down.

◗ You can't find your keys anywhere.

◗ You don't read the small print on a document and later find out it has cost you dearly.

◗ You buy something expensive and find out it's half-price in the sale a couple of weeks later or cheaper elsewhere.

▶ Your computer crashes and you lose all your work.

▶ Documents don't reach the intended recipient, or your phone call or text message goes unanswered.

▶ Your flight is delayed or your luggage goes missing.

▶ You turn up to the wrong restaurant when meeting a friend.

▶ Your workmate forgets you've arranged a meeting and doesn't turn up.

▶ Your pay gets directed to the wrong bank account.

▶ You have an argument with your best friend because they think you've been gossiping about them.

▶ You get stuck in a traffic jam or your car breaks down.

Of course, all these things happen when Mercury isn't retrograde, it's just that they seem to do so more frequently when it is. All of this is inconvenient, annoying and frustrating, and the best thing you can do is plan ahead and be extra mindful of Mercury's influence. And, of course, things can also go right during Mercury's retrograde period. For example:

◗ An old friend gets back in touch.

◗ You finally finish the work project that's been driving you mad.

◗ A gadget breaks down, but you get a new and better one.

◗ You renegotiate an agreement in your favour.

◗ You have to redo a project and, in doing so, improve it out of sight.

◗ You need to have a tricky conversation you've avoided, but it works out well.

◗ Something you'd been looking for turns up.

◗ You find the purse you'd lost *and* it's got more cash in it than you remember.

◗ Your redecorating projects turn out better than you hoped.

◗ Your website crashes and you replace it with a much better site.

◗ You return a dress you bought because you don't like the colour and have no problems getting a refund.

◗ Your dreams bring you an insight into a problem.

However, like all planetary patterns, Mercury retrograde is likely to affect you more strongly if it connects with your birth chart. For example, if you were born under Aries and Mercury is going retrograde in Aries, it's likely to affect you more strongly than someone born under the sign of Cancer (unless that person has, say, a Cancer Moon and Mercury retrogrades right over it, of course).

Also, if you have Mercury retrograde in your birth chart, you might not feel the effects of Mercury retrograde as much as others, because you're more accustomed to it. Some people born with Mercury retrograde claim that Mercury retrograde later in life actually works in their favour and makes them feel normal (*see pages 27–29*).

Generally, as with everything in life, whether things go right or wrong depends a lot on how you react to the Mercury retrograde energy. If you take an extra second to hang up your keys by the door when you arrive home, read important documents several times and are a bit more forgiving when a friend says something particularly daft, you're likely to have fewer problems. Even things that look like they could be an unmitigated disaster, such as running into your ex, might not be as awful as you think. Perhaps you can see it as a chance for a catch-up chat about old friends. And that's the point: if you're open to the opportunities that present themselves, but don't rush into judgement, then you can make the best of Mercury retrograde.

Due to the concentrated planetary energies during the retrograde, it's likely that expressing yourself clearly is more of a challenge than usual – but it isn't impossible. You may just need to focus more and listen harder. You may also find that the retrograde period isn't the best time to launch something new; however, you can do that later once you've worked out all your options.

However, the myth that Mercury retrograde will bring havoc, torment and misery is just that – a myth. Yes, things are different under Mercury retrograde, and yes, you'll have challenges to deal with but, as we said previously, Mercury is a trickster and once you've learned about his tricks, you can turn them to your advantage.

The three passes of Mercury retrograde

If you're new to astrology, you may not have heard about how retrograde cycles work symbolically and might like to equate it to the following idea:

When you're born, you have no idea that you can't drive a car – you're **unconsciously unskilled**. Quite soon though, you do become aware that you can't drive a car (say by three or four years old, or sooner if you're a real bright spark!) – you're now **consciously unskilled**. Eventually, most likely around 16 or 17 years of age, depending on where you live, you start to learn how to drive a car. You can do it, but as you learn, you have to think about everything – braking, turning, parking, etc – you're now **consciously skilled**. Finally, after a few months or years of driving, it all starts to flow. You can drive around without thinking about whether you should change gears, indicate, brake, etc – you're now **unconsciously skilled**. You're skilled to the point of being able to drive without thinking too hard about it.

Retrogrades are a bit like that: they have what's called 'three passes'.

The planet is moving forwards in one House of your chart and may trigger one or more of your planets as it goes (*see Part IV for more about this*). This is the **first pass**. You deal with whatever it brings up. You're unconsciously unskilled.

The planet then starts to go retrograde (or appears to) and, as it retraces its steps in your chart, you can get some echoes or even repeats in your life and past themes reappear. What you experience is based on where the retrograde is taking place for you – which sign, which House and which planets it's triggering. This can be quite an intense part of the cycle, as you get a double dose of the planet: a second chance perhaps, or a reminder that you didn't quite get something right the first time around and here's another, possibly last (for now), chance. This is the **second pass**. You're hopefully becoming consciously skilled.

Finally, the retrograde ends. The planet has gone as far back in your chart as it's going to for now and resumes its forwards motion. Once again, the planet goes over the same part of your chart, triggering everything all over again, and again quite possibly bringing up some of the same issues and life themes that came up during the first two passes. This is the final pass of the retrograde. Ideally, this time around, you've learned how to deal with the issues this transit is teaching you and now barely notice them. You know how to deal with the retrograde. This is the **third pass**. You're now unconsciously skilled.

Using Mercury retrograde to your advantage

Make no mistake, Mercury retrograde can also be used very consciously. Yoko Ono famously chose to sign contracts under Mercury retrograde so she could more easily renegotiate them later.

I, Yasmin, once bought an apartment at auction under Mercury retrograde but then realized the mortgage broker had arranged a 90 per cent variable mortgage on it – which wasn't what I had asked for and it worried me terribly. However, knowing that Mercury was retrograde, I simply found another broker and got a new mortgage, all before the first payment was taken out of my account and with no penalties!

We believe Mercury retrograde is the Universe's way of saying that you're not yet ready to decide; there are other factors you don't know about, for which you need to account, so keep gathering the facts.

Some people like to try and put their life on hold when Mercury is retrograde. However, that isn't very realistic. Who can put their life on hold for weeks? But, of course, if you do have the chance to retreat under Mercury retrograde for a while, grab it with both hands because it's an ideal time to take a break and recharge your batteries.

Similarly, if you're planning to travel under Mercury retrograde, it's best to make all the arrangements you can in advance. Otherwise, though, and overall, be kind to yourself. You might have to slow down for a while, but if you stay focused and get ready to enjoy what Mercury retrograde has to offer, you can minimize any potential problems.

As we described earlier, the effect of Mercury retrograde is strongest during the shadow phases, when it first turns retrograde and when it changes direction to become direct again. However, it will have an effect on the world for the whole time it's retrograde, as well as just before and just after.

The bottom line of the Mercury retrograde is:

◗ Don't assume everything will go wrong during Mercury retrograde – sometimes it will work in your favour; for example, if you turn down a job because the salary is too low, the employer might come back to you with a better offer.

◗ When Mercury retrograde brings old issues to the surface, remember to use it as an opportunity to tidy up anything you've left unresolved in the past. Once you've done that, you can collect your ideas and figure out what you're going to do next. At the very least, Mercury retrograde is a great excuse to get organized.

◗ This isn't the right time to start something new, but you can improve what you already have or complete any unfinished projects. If you *do* have to start something new, guess what? You'll probably restart it or end it under a future Mercury retrograde.

● Even if you try, you'll find it hard to nail down a plan. Be aware that it may be hard to get decisions from others – and any decisions that are made will likely be subject to change once Mercury turns direct.

● Sometimes, close relationships can be problematic under Mercury retrograde: for example, there can be miscommunication and your loved one could announce dramatically that they're off and will never darken your door again – only to return the following week. That's because people aren't always thinking straight at this time.

The best way to take advantage of the Mercury retrograde is to focus on the prefix **re–** (which implies repetition), and focus on the following:

Renew

If you take on new commitments before dealing with old ones, you could become overloaded. Renew your current commitments and see them through.

Review

We all need time to review things and decide whether we're taking the right road. Maybe it's time for a new approach. Double-checking everything might seem to slow things down, but it could save you time and grief in the long run. Reviewing your financial arrangements, for example, could save you a small fortune; you might be able to get a better deal from a different utility company or switch to a credit card with a lower interest rate, if you look into it under Mercury retrograde.

Reflect

Sometimes you need to take time out to consider your next move. Mercury retrograde is a time to reflect on what you've accomplished so far and where you want to redirect your energies. You might be more intuitive and aware of your unconscious thoughts during Mercury retrograde and discover insights that are usually blocked by conscious thought.

Revise

Although it can be frustrating if a meeting is cancelled or postponed, it allows you to gather additional information that may come in handy – or simply recharge your batteries so you can get more out of it. Similarly, it's a great time to revise a written project.

Revamp

If something you own is looking a bit outdated, the easy option is to go shopping to replace it. But with minimal effort you might be able to transform it into something new. Mercury retrograde is a brilliant time for upcycling.

Repair

It's easy to be lazy about repairs but that small leak can lead to a major flood if you don't get it fixed, so gather your resources and plan to make good any domestic repairs.

Rethink

As your life changes, so do your ideas. This is a great time to review your beliefs, standards and perceptions and whether any of them are due to habit rather than your current reality.

Refrain

If you don't succumb to an impulse buy, you give yourself the time to find what you want at a cheaper price – maybe even to find something that suits you better.

Research

Part of taking any action is ensuring you have all the information you need at your fingertips. You can make your final decision once Mercury is direct again.

Return

In terms of work, going back to old customers and clients can make better business sense than spending your energy on making new contacts.

Revisit

There might be somewhere you keep intending to return, but somehow you never have the time. You can make the time under Mercury retrograde. Or you might want to revisit an old situation and see it with fresh eyes.

Reorganize

If you're surrounded by clutter, it's hard to get anything done. Taking time out to organize your home, your workspace and your life will pay enormous dividends in the long term.

Retrieve

Lost items often come to light under Mercury retrograde, especially if you spend your time clearing out clutter.

Reconnect

Reconnecting with friends and relatives can be one of the most positive sides of Mercury's retrograde period.

However, if you reconnect with an ex, you might want to hold back because there's usually a very good reason why they're now an ex. You can also reconnect with your goals and put your mind to achieving them.

Resolve

Even if you ignore them, unresolved arguments are there in the background and affect your relationships. Bringing any conflicts into the open and dealing with them will allow everyone to make a fresh start.

Repeat

Although it might be frustrating, it's much better to repeat yourself to make sure you've been understood than deal with problems later. People might not be on the same wavelength as you, so don't make assumptions.

Be prepared: dos and don'ts for Mercury retrograde

As we've described, Mercury retrograde is a great time to deal with unfinished business. We all start things we don't get around to completing, creating clutter in our lives. This period gives us time to tie up loose ends and create a clear vision for the future. If you take advantage of it, you'll be ready for what's next when Mercury goes direct. That's why part of making the most of Mercury retrograde is being prepared.

Use the quick checklist of dos and don'ts below to help you make the right decisions.

Do	Don't
Read everything at least twice before signing or you might miss something in the details. If you sign a document during this time, you may change your mind or want to tweak the terms or conditions when Mercury turns direct.	Sign documents without reading all the small print. This obviously applies all the time, but especially when Mercury is retrograde.
Renegotiate existing agreements.	Make new agreements or life-altering decisions that you want to be absolutely set in stone (because they won't be).
Expect delays and even cancellations when travelling. You might not be able to avoid travelling, so allow extra time in case of cancellations, postponements and delays.	Travel without a back-up plan and check everything in advance. Pack your sense of humour along with everything else. (Mercury is the trickster!)

Do	Don't
Allow plenty of time to deal with possible delays when travelling for appointments. Reconfirm the details before you set off.	Leave late for appointments and expect to make it on time. You're more likely to end up doubly late than to arrive on time.
Renew your commitments instead of making new ones. Finish things you started a while ago.	Start anything new before finishing what's on your to-do list. Otherwise you might have to redo things later.
Compare prices for something you plan to buy later and get repairs done on what you already own. If you do buy something, keep your receipt. Reduce your clutter and give away any old items.	Make major purchases, especially a car or computer, if you can possibly avoid it. That said, if you do buy something big now, you'll likely replace it under a future Mercury retrograde cycle.
Reapply for a job. Rewrite your CV.	Start a new job without being prepared for a few false starts and restarts. It may take some time for it to work out smoothly – but you'll learn.

Do	Don't
Return to a course of study you didn't complete.	Start a new course, if you can avoid it. On the upside, anything started under Mercury retrograde should be easily tweaked and reworked to suit your needs.
Keep your mobile charged and back up your digital data.	Rely on your gadgets – it's easier to mislay your mobile or fall prey to a computer virus while Mercury is retrograde.
Get together with old friends and expect to hear from, or run into, people from your past at the weirdest moments. Double-check and confirm all dates, plans, meetings, appointments in advance.	Get together or schedule a meeting with an ex without careful thought. You're more likely to experience confusion, mistakes and cancellations, or an on-again/off-again romance. Romances that start under Mercury retrograde will be forever under the influence of the cycle – but that can work well. You'll have to test it and see!

Do	Don't
Read all emails and documents before you send them.	Send an email without double-checking – you could hit 'reply all' or send it to the wrong person. Send in unchecked work. This is another 'rule' that always applies but applies double under Mercury retrograde.
Pause and breathe before speaking. Repeat yourself if necessary.	Lead people on, give mixed messages or believe everything you hear (actions speak louder than words), jump to conclusions, or spread rumours.

If things do go wrong when Mercury is retrograde, try not to assume the worst. Give other people the benefit of the doubt. People, you included, are likely to be more careless, mistake-prone and forgetful when Mercury is retrograde; someone might not have read your e-mail or text – the fact that they haven't yet replied doesn't necessarily mean they're ignoring you. Sometimes having conversations face to face can make things easier.

Be aware that anything started or purchased during Mercury retrograde may need to be revisited and revised at least once before you get what you want from it, whether it's a new job, a new phone or whatever. It will be worth the revisiting and revisions because Mercury is a teacher.

If you're frustrated or confused by a retrograde cycle, it may help to remember that all your fellow earthlings are similarly afflicted; try to be kind and tolerant to yourself and to others.

Mercury's retrograde cycles present us with opportunities to recoup our investments of time, money and attention. No matter when we start something, Mercury retrograde will present us with a way to revisit, review and repair it.

The golden rule

The key with Mercury retrograde is always to let the cycle unfold without making any major decisions, if you can. Mercury retrograde usually leads to more information being sent your way, so it's best to see what transpires and, if possible, wait until the end of the cycle (and ideally a few days after that) before you act.

How to use this book

This book is divided into four parts that explore how Mercury retrograde is likely to manifest in your life, what to avoid and how to make the best of it.

Part I explains how Mercury retrograde is likely to play out for you depending on the element in which Mercury is retrograding (Fire, Earth, Air or Water). In Part II we look at how Mercury retrograde affects each of the 12 zodiac or Star signs, and in Part III we explain how Mercury retrograde manifests its energies through the 12 Houses of your birth chart. Part IV looks at what happens when Mercury retrograde meets your planets. That's followed by an Appendix listing of Mercury retrograde dates for the next 10 years.

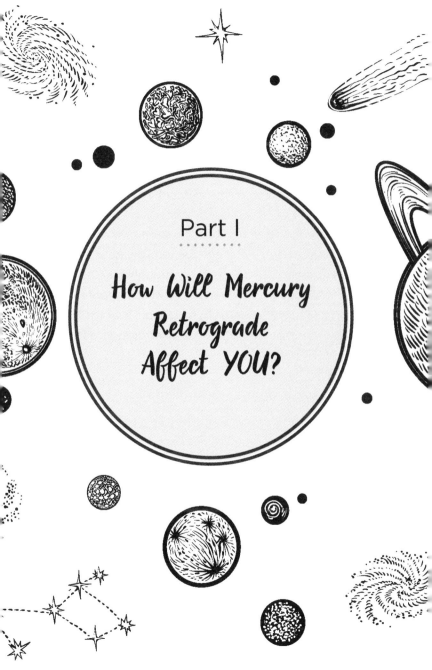

Part I

How Will Mercury Retrograde Affect YOU?

You need to ask four questions to find out how a particular Mercury retrograde is likely to play out for you:

1. Which element is Mercury retrograde in?

2. Which sign is Mercury retrograde in?

3. Which part of my chart (which House) is it retrograde in?

4. Is it triggering any of my planets? (Although this is more for student astrologers.)

While simply knowing that Mercury is retrograde is enough to warn you that things will be a little different, if you also know which **element** and **sign** it's retrograde in, you'll have a lot of useful information. Add to that which part of your personal chart it's in and which planets it's triggering, and you'll have the full picture. You can glean all that information from this book.

To find out where and when Mercury is retrograde, you can simply keep an eye on newspaper and online columns or your Facebook feed for updates. Or if you prefer to plan ahead you can refer to the Appendix, which gives the dates of Mercury retrograde for the next 10 years (*see pages 179–182*).

The retrograde symbol

You might have noticed that a retrograde planet has its own special symbol (℞) which looks like the letter R with its tail crossed by a line. Sometimes it's written as Rx for simplicity on a keyboard, though this is just a convenient approximation. Mercury retrograde is indicated by the symbol for Mercury (☿) followed by the retrograde symbol (℞). As well as being the symbol for a retrograde planet, ℞ is also the symbol for prescription, as used by doctors and pharmacists, and comes from the Latin word *recipe*, meaning 'take'.

There are theories regarding the origin of ℞. One is that it was adapted from the symbol for Jupiter (♃), as an invocation to God. However, this might simply be due to printers using the Jupiter symbol in place of ℞. Another theory is that it's adapted from the Egyptian Eye of Horus, shown opposite.

The Eye of Horus

This symbol was used in Ancient Egypt to ward off evil, protect the king in the afterlife and for good health; there's little evidence for this theory, although an eye has been used as a symbol for pharmacies.

The first theory – that it was adapted from the symbol for Jupiter – is most likely. A number of single letter abbreviations have been amended by adding a single stroke – for example, £ actually is a letter 'L' with a horizontal dash to indicate 'pound' (*libra* in Latin).

Mercury Retrograde Through the Elements

Each time Mercury goes retrograde, it stops at an earlier degree in the zodiac than the previous time – which means its retrograde cycle gradually moves further back. Over the long term, this means that after Mercury is retrograde in a Water sign, it will next be retrograde in an Air sign, followed by an Earth and then a Fire sign. Mercury often begins by being retrograde in one sign and then ends in another. The pattern isn't regular, but Mercury is least often retrograde in a Water sign. That's partly why Mercury retrograde in a Water sign can be harder for people to cope with – they're less familiar with it.

Mercury is only retrograde for about three weeks at a time, but it can spend up to three months in the same sign when you include the shadow phases (see *page xvi*). That means a lot of emphasis on everything associated with that sign – which in turn gives us plenty of time to rethink and review.

Going backwards doesn't have to be a negative, because sometimes we need more time to think something through again, to pause and/or take stock. In fact, stepping back to reflect is often followed by a more productive phase because it makes it easier to reach the right decision. The best solution is to gather all the information you can about your most pressing issue while Mercury is retrograde but wait until the cycle is over before making any decisions or taking action.

The big picture

In some ways, the best place to start in terms of interpreting what each Mercury retrograde cycle is likely to herald is by looking at the elements. As you might know, in astrology we break the 12 zodiac signs down into four elements: Fire, Earth, Air and Water. Here's a list of them:

▶ **Fire signs:** Aries, Leo and Sagittarius

▶ **Earth signs:** Taurus, Virgo and Capricorn

▶ **Air signs:** Gemini, Libra and Aquarius

▶ **Water signs:** Cancer, Scorpio and Pisces

The three zodiac signs in an element have a lot in common so we can actually draw some broad brushstrokes for everyone, regardless of their Star sign or Rising sign, about what it means when Mercury is retrograde in one of the four elements.

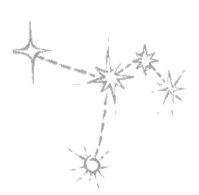

Mercury Retrograde in a Fire Sign

Aries, Leo or Sagittarius

···━━━━━━━━━━━━━━━━━━━━━━━━━━━━━━━···

When Mercury goes retrograde in a Fire sign, it can feel like a bit of a damp squib. You may be eager to do amazing things – after all, fire energy lights up the world, it's creative and even flashy – but under this cycle there are tedious delays to deal with. Or maybe you just need more time to birth your creation.

Fire energy gives off sparks, but you need to ask, 'Is this really what I want to do? Can I carry it through to the end?' Honestly? No one's testing you. You're allowed to give up and start again if you want!

Fire is also all about burning brightly, but Mercury retrograde in a Fire sign can delude you into thinking you're 'on fire' when in reality you're simply following an urge to do anything other than sit still. Instead you need to reach within to feel the burn of your inner flame – it's there, even if you haven't fanned it for a while. And that's another thing – if life's been dragging you down, Mercury retrograde in a Fire sign encourages you to learn how to play again.

Don't be shy about being more creative in making life changes. Fire signs live life large, so ask yourself if you're enjoying your life journey as much as possible. Whatever you do under this cycle, you may have a couple of false starts, but each experience will help you to unleash your creativity a little bit more.

Working with Mercury's energies

Working with fire is the easiest way to harness Mercury's energies in a practical or sacred way. Whether you simply light a candle and meditate or invite friends to join you at a fire pit and light up some flames, any ritual involving fire is a great way of connecting with the energies of Mercury retrograde in a Fire sign.

Good for...

Thinking about how you develop your creative side and follow your true passions.

Benefits...

Anyone with their Sun or Rising sign in a Fire sign or, to a lesser extent, an Air sign.

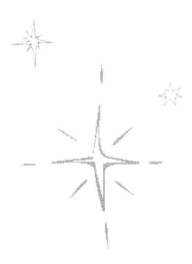

Mercury Retrograde in an Earth Sign

Taurus, Virgo or Capricorn

• • • ──────────────────────────────── • • •

When Mercury is retrograde in an Earth sign, the energy is, of course, more 'down to earth' and even a bit more serious. It's time to reconnect with Mother Earth. Spend time outdoors and/or reviewing what you can do to protect the environment. Do you need something new or can you fix (or fix up) things you already have? Having a less disposable lifestyle can benefit the planet and your wallet.

Practical matters are likely to be on your mind – it's time to review the basics. If you need to be more organized, that's likely to become very clear now. If you don't make changes, they might be thrust on you – it's much better to be prepared.

In a typically quirky Mercury retrograde way, once you're more organized, it becomes a lot easier to be more spontaneous and enjoy the fun things in life. But to start with, when Mercury is retrograde in an Earth sign, pay attention to doing things on time, sticking to your budget and looking after your health. Money can be both the problem and the solution under this cycle.

If you run a business, Mercury retrograde in an Earth sign is a great time for reconnecting with old clients or following up on business leads. If you can persuade yourself to be a little more flexible and adaptable, you'll spot even more new opportunities.

Working with Mercury's energies

Anything that comes from the earth forms the basis of a great ritual while Mercury is retrograde in an Earth sign. For example, you could use sacred stones, crystals and flowers to create a beautiful mandala while you ask the heavens to show you what you need to learn.

Good for...

Re-evaluating your goals. It's also a really good time to get back down to earth, if you know you've been a bit scatty or flaky. If you like to work with crystals, now is the time to give them all a really good cleanse, recharge and re-programme.

Benefits...

Anyone with their Sun or Rising sign in an Earth sign or, to a lesser extent, in a Water sign.

Mercury Retrograde in an Air Sign

Gemini, Libra or Aquarius

··· ———————————————————————————— ···

I f you can both pay attention and become aware, you can make connections and have 'aha' moments during this time. Life is often an experiment, and we need theories to test and revise.

This is a good time for doing yoga and breathwork to counteract the 'monkey mind' that comes with jumbled thoughts and lack of focus.

When Mercury is retrograde in an Air sign, there'll also be plenty of befuddled ideas and confusing chatter, so avoid too much talking that doesn't go anywhere. You've got your thinking cap on, but is it on backwards? You might even be wearing a selection of thinking caps, each one leading your mind in a different direction.

That said, airing your thoughts can be really productive now; it gives ideas a second life, resolves misunderstandings and encourages others to share their ideas with you, too. Do keep reminding yourself to listen as well as talk.

There may be a lot of minor irritations while Mercury is retrograde in an Air sign. For example, you might lose documents, miss your train or spend hours waiting for a friend who's forgotten they're supposed to meet you. It's also not a great time to buy machinery such as cars or computers.

Life will be easier if you keep things simple. The more things you try to do, the easier it is for them to go wrong. And try not to make hasty decisions when Mercury is retrograde in an Air sign because you might not have all the information you need.

Working with Mercury's energies

Rituals to connect with Mercury retrograde are a great way to tune in to the cycle rather than fighting against it – which can be the natural inclination. To work with the element of air, a beautiful bird's feather (symbolizing flight) would work well, as would a ritual that involves journaling (because the element of air is all about ideas).

Good for...

Talking things through or catching up with correspondence, and it's a good time to be on Facebook or other social media. However, be aware that social media mix-ups are a bit more likely at this time. If you have kids, it's a good time to do a spot check on their social media to ensure all is well in their cyberworld.

Benefits...

Anyone with their Sun or Rising sign in an Air sign or, to a lesser extent, in a Fire sign.

Mercury Retrograde in a Water Sign

Cancer, Scorpio or Pisces

...————————————————————...

You need to follow your instincts when Mercury is retrograde in a Water sign. This is a time to listen to that small voice within – especially if it starts shouting. It isn't so much what's said to you that matters now as the way it's said – a smile in someone's eyes is worth much more than a smile on their face. It's also a time to revisit old emotions – maybe for purging, maybe for soothing.

This is a good time to slow down, home in on your emotional reactions and ask yourself what you're feeling, and why. It's wise to be non-judgemental and kind to yourself and others. It may help to realize that it isn't just you who's running high on emotion – Mercury retrograde is affecting everyone.

You might feel like stepping back and taking time out to gather your thoughts. Gaining some perspective can help you see how old habits have been holding you back and how you can change them.

Analysing your dreams and feelings and keeping a journal are great ways to reap the full benefits of Mercury retrograde in a Water sign. You're likely to be more intuitive, sensitive and imaginative, so all you need to do is recognize exactly how. You can get insights into the past now too.

Working with Mercury's energies

When Mercury is 'reversing' in a Water sign it will often be an extra emotional cycle. Tune in to the energies and befriend them by working with the element of water. For example, use a beautiful goblet or chalice filled with filtered water and speak any worries you have around the Mercury retrograde cycle into the cup before pouring it away (preferably into the earth).

Good for...

Spending time alone in contemplation. It's also a really good time to feel any feelings you previously supressed because you couldn't handle them. For example, if you went through something traumatic and have blocked out the memory, you might now feel more equipped to work through your emotions so that they don't fester and become toxic.

Benefits

Anyone with their Sun or Rising sign in a Water sign or, to a lesser extent, in an Earth sign.

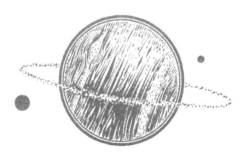

What If You Were Born Under Mercury Retrograde?

So, what if you were born when Mercury was retrograde? To check, simply cast your chart for free at www.theastrologybook.com/freechart and look for the ℞ symbol next to the Mercury glyph (☿) for your date of birth (*see also page 4*).

Far from being an affliction, it's likely that you cope better with Mercury retrograde than other people, especially when Mercury is retrograde in the same element as in your birth chart.

If you have problems with expression and communication, then it's likely to improve each time Mercury turns retrograde. And while other people are more muddled and confused, you might find that your senses sharpen and you're able to make more sense of the world. In fact, having Mercury retrograde in your birth chart usually doesn't mean that your mind is weaker but often the exact opposite.

There may be times when you feel that you need to reject your mental energy and power because you're overwhelmed, or because you've had so much negative feedback from other people that you sense there must be something wrong with you. Chances are that you're fine, you just think differently and it can take a while to develop confidence in your mental abilities, ideas and opinions.

Some people with Mercury retrograde in their birth chart may struggle with thinking and communication; speaking, writing or feeling misunderstood. Their communication skills often get easier as they grow up though, and learn ways of expressing themselves through writing, art, music or dance. You may also find that you process information differently to your friends and find it harder to put things into words. This means that some people might see you as quiet or shy.

If you find communication tricky then traditional methods of learning might not suit you, although chances are you manage to struggle your way through them. For this reason, artistic and creative outlets can be beneficial to you, so if you're still having issues this is worth exploring.

You may rely more strongly on your intuition than others and like to take your time when it comes to making decisions. You might also find it difficult to be objective about your own ideas because you can't separate yourself from them and get a more detached perspective.

In general terms, you absorb thoughts and ideas through osmosis and tend to accept what others say without question. You're also probably more capable of dealing with abstractions than most people. It's possible that you're a reflective person who likes to explore ideas.

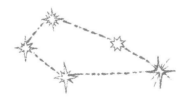

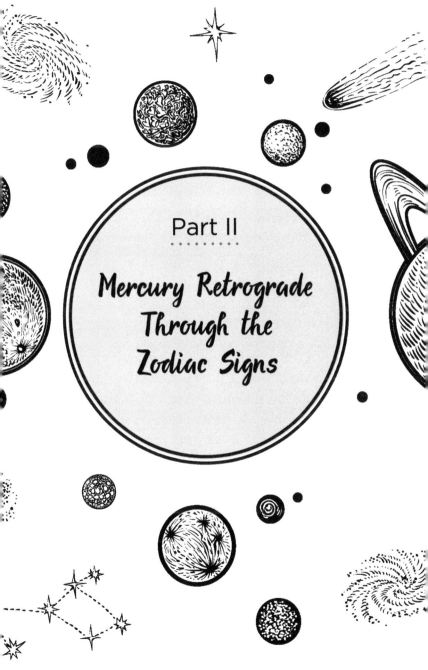

Part II

Mercury Retrograde
Through the
Zodiac Signs

Although some factors are common to Mercury retrograde whichever sign it's in, Mercury does act differently in different signs. Similarly, although Mercury in, say, a Fire sign manifests as described in Part I, there's a slight difference between whether it's in Aries, Leo or Sagittarius. And when Mercury is retrograde in the same sign as your Sun or Rising sign, it will have a stronger effect on you.

In this section you'll find general information about what Mercury retrograde means through the 12 signs of the zodiac. You can read this section without considering what the retrograde means for you personally – that is, without knowing which part of your own chart the retrograde is taking place in – as the information is relevant for everyone, regardless of their Star sign or Rising sign.

All you need to know to use it is the sign in which Mercury is retrograding. You can find this out by referring to the Appendix (*see pages 179–182*) or by visiting www.yasminboland.com. You might even like to make a note of the dates in your diary so you're prepared in advance!

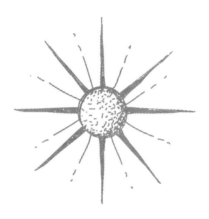

The Upside of Mercury Retrograde in Aries

When Mercury is retrograde in Aries, the best possible upside has to be that we all get a second chance to be brave. So, if you chickened out of something, Mercury retrograde in the impulsive first sign of the zodiac is giving you a second chance to be gutsy.

Aries represents the fearless and innocent infant for whom everything is fresh and new. Try to be less cynical and more aware of the everyday wonders of this marvellous world.

By the end of this cycle, once you've become clearer on whatever has been perplexing you, you should finally be able to find the courage to deal with things you've been procrastinating about – including sharing the truth with someone.

However, you need to choose your words carefully under this cycle because it's harder to hold back from saying what you really think.

The Aries energy is usually very speedy but here we have a slowing down. It's as though there's a message coming to us from the heavens saying, 'Take it easy, it's not a race...' For that reason, it's a very good time to learn the benefits that come from thinking first and speaking later, rather than the other way around.

Five things to do

◗ Look before you leap.

◗ Stop talking and start listening.

◗ Re-find your chutzpah.

◗ Reassess recent decisions.

◗ Focus on motivating yourself rather than those around you.

Watch out for...

It's all too easy to jump to conclusions under this cycle. Many of us are going to feel that we have an answer to everything ... but it might not be the right answer. In fact, sometimes there's more than one way of being right, so don't get all shouty and stomp up and down if someone disagrees with you – it isn't necessarily personal. Take your time when you speak and check no one's getting the wrong end of the stick, because it can take ages to unravel misunderstandings.

Most issues raised by Mercury retrograde in Aries can be resolved by slowing down.

How Mercury retrograde affects you

▶ Aries or Aries rising: it's in your 1st House (*see page 89*)

▶ Taurus or Taurus rising: it's in your 12th House (*see page 153*)

▶ Gemini or Gemini rising: it's in your 11th House (*see page 149*)

▶ Cancer or Cancer rising: it's in your 10th House (*see page 143*)

▶ Leo or Leo rising: it's in your 9th House (*see page 137*)

▶ Virgo or Virgo rising: it's in your 8th House (*see page 131*)

▶ Libra or Libra rising: it's in your 7th House (*see page 125*)

▶ Scorpio or Scorpio rising: it's in your 6th House (*see page 119*)

▶ Sagittarius or Sagittarius rising: it's in your 5th House (*see page 113*)

▶ Capricorn or Capricorn rising: it's in your 4th House (*see page 107*)

▶ Aquarius or Aquarius rising: it's in your 3rd House (*see page 101*)

▶ Pisces or Pisces rising: it's in your 2nd House (*see page 95*)

The Upside of Mercury Retrograde in Taurus

Mercury retrograde in Taurus is a time to remember what makes life worth living. Once you rethink what really matters to you, it's only a small step to bring it back into your life.

Taurus is associated with money and values, so if you've wandered off the path in terms of living a life (or earning a living) in accordance with your values, this is the time to get back on track.

Mercury retrograde can also bring second chances related to cash, property and possessions. And this can also be a time to return to a more sensual way of living.

You've got the vision, now you need to add some substance to it.

Five things to do

◗ Get a massage and/or bring back sensuality.

◗ Review your finances and pay off loans.

◗ Remember what really matters.

◗ Stop and smell the flowers.

◗ Get back to nature.

Watch out for...

There's a difference between being lazy and taking your time, but the line is a fine one. A bit more flexibility will help, so try not to be too rigid in your thinking. Sometimes it's better to yield to others.

This isn't a great time to start anything new, especially if you start skipping steps to save time. Hold back a while and be patient with others.

Money matters in particular can cause problems when Mercury is retrograde in Taurus, so allow extra time for compromise and last-minute details. Paying attention to the finer details and asking questions when necessary will help protect you against financial crises. Being careful with your money is great – but you need to avoid being mean. It really isn't the same thing.

An old lover from the past could reappear, thanks to Taurus' association with Venus and sensuality. Remember, there's a reason why they're part of your past.

How Mercury retrograde affects you

▶ Aries or Aries rising: it's in your 2nd House (*see page 95*)

▶ Taurus or Taurus rising: it's in your 1st House (*see page 89*)

▶ Gemini or Gemini rising: it's in your 12th House (*see page 153*)

▶ Cancer or Cancer rising: it's in your 11th House (*see page 149*)

▶ Leo or Leo rising: it's in your 10th House (*see page 143*)

▶ Virgo or Virgo rising: it's in your 9th House (*see page 137*)

▶ Libra or Libra rising: it's in your 8th House (*see page 131*)

▶ Scorpio or Scorpio rising: it's in your 7th House (*see page 125*)

◗ Sagittarius or Sagittarius rising: it's in your 6th House (*see page 119*)

◗ Capricorn or Capricorn rising: it's in your 5th House (*see page 113*)

◗ Aquarius or Aquarius rising: it's in your 4th House (*see page 107*)

◗ Pisces or Pisces rising: it's in your 3rd House (*see page 101*)

♊

The Upside of Mercury Retrograde in Gemini

Asking questions is fine as long as you listen to the answers. This is a great time for reviewing information – it will be easier to join the dots once the retrograde is over. Speak slowly and listen harder.

Reflecting on past experiences can show you the way forwards now, too. You might need to think things through again before you make your final decision, but you're happy to take as long as it takes.

Mercury retrograde in Gemini encourages us to slow down and connect the dots. The connections don't come as quickly, nor the responses as glibly. The immediate reply won't be the final answer; fine-tuning (possibly prompted by new information) will be needed to get you from Point A to Point B.

You're likely to be surrounded by gossip, too, but this needn't be a bad thing. It can be fun raking over the past with friends and updating each other on the latest news. Sharing what you know can make your world run more smoothly – so as long as you remember that *some* juicy facts are meant to be kept secret.

Five things to do

▶ Back up your computer.

▶ Apologize to anyone you've offended, especially a sibling.

▶ Take a break.

▶ Edit a writing project rather than forge ahead.

▶ Catch up on reading you've been meaning to do for eons.

Watch out for...

Retrograde Mercury in Gemini can cause communication mayhem. Somehow, words seem to take on a whole new meaning – it can feel like you and the person you're talking to are actually speaking different languages (when you're not!). And you might get the wrong end of the stick when someone tells you something. It's worth checking and rechecking anything you're told. Other people tend to be more critical than usual – but here's a top tip: you probably don't need to point out absolutely everything that's wrong.

There can be last-minute cancellations, missed and/or garbled messages, and possible car or computer issues. Save your money for the time being and don't go shopping for electronic items if you can avoid it. Mercury retrograde in Gemini is like a double dose, since Gemini is one of Mercury's home signs.

Travel plans are also prone to delays or complications and major moves can be a source of regret. Boring as it might sound, it's best to stay put as much as possible. Alternatively, you could see it as 'meant to be' if your plans are thrown into chaos and change.

This retrograde Mercury sometimes brings out scammers and con artists so, if it sounds too good to be true, then it probably is. If someone promises you the Moon, make sure it's actually their Moon before you strike a deal.

How Mercury retrograde affects you

▶ Aries or Aries rising: it's in your 3rd House (*see page 101*)

▶ Taurus or Taurus rising: it's in your 2nd House (*see page 95*)

▶ Gemini or Gemini rising: it's in your 1st House (*see page 89*)

▶ Cancer or Cancer rising: it's in your 12th House (*see page 153*)

▶ Leo or Leo rising: it's in your 11th House (*see page 149*)

▶ Virgo or Virgo rising: it's in your 10th House (*see page 143*)

▶ Libra or Libra rising: it's in your 9th House (*see page 137*)

▶ Scorpio or Scorpio rising: it's in your 8th House (*see page 131*)

▶ Sagittarius or Sagittarius rising: it's in your 7th House (*see page 125*)

▶ Capricorn or Capricorn rising: it's in your 6th House (*see page 119*)

▶ Aquarius or Aquarius rising: it's in your 5th House (*see page 113*)

▶ Pisces or Pisces rising: it's in your 4th House (*see page 107*)

The Upside of Mercury Retrograde in Cancer

This is a great time for redoing any domestic activities. A spring clean will make your home a lot more sparkly than it usually would, as you're prepared to stick at it until everything is shiny, shiny. It's also a time when you might decide to or actually renovate. That's fine, but keep a close eye on the details – for example, if you order a particular item, make sure you get what you ordered not something similar but wrong.

Along the same home and family lines, if you haven't seen much of your family recently, now is the time to get back in touch. Maybe a quick call to one or two family members is all that's needed, but you could go the whole hog and arrange a party or meal out. You could all have a superb time!

A beautiful use of Mercury retrograde in Cancer is to get together with people you love and share your happiest memories. This cycle also makes it easier to offer good quality advice to your loved ones based on past experiences.

Five things to do

- Hold or plan a family reunion and/or research the family tree.
- Work on home repairs and/or redecorating.
- Review or rethink your diet and improve your cookery skills.
- Revise your plans for achieving the family life you want and need.
- Read biographies or history books, or watch a historical drama or documentary series.

Watch out for...

We can all feel a lot more sensitive while Mercury is retrograde in Cancer. So much so, that it's too easy to read the worst into everything everyone says - even subjects you usually couldn't care less about can become sensitive. If you don't want to get into an argument, simply walk quietly away.

Also, it's worth heeding this warning: trying to manipulate people emotionally with what you say may backfire. It's better to be straight dealing, especially if you feel a little befuddled and want to ignore facts that contradict your feelings.

Maybe your home life isn't perfect at this point – or maybe it's simply that you're more tuned in to what's wrong. But deciding to move at this point isn't a great idea – wait to make any decision like this until after the retrograde, otherwise there's a fair chance you'll take your problems with you.

How Mercury retrograde affects you

▶ Aries or Aries rising: it's in your 4th House (*see page 107*)

▶ Taurus or Taurus rising: it's in your 3rd House (*see page 101*)

▶ Gemini or Gemini rising: it's in your 2nd House (*see page 95*)

▶ Cancer or Cancer rising: it's in your 1st House (*see page 89*)

▶ Leo or Leo rising: it's in your 12th House (*see page 153*)

- Virgo or Virgo rising: it's in your 11th House (*see page 149*)

- Libra or Libra rising: it's in your 10th House (*see page 143*)

- Scorpio or Scorpio rising: it's in your 9th House (*see page 137*)

- Sagittarius or Sagittarius rising: it's in your 8th House (*see page 131*)

- Capricorn or Capricorn rising: it's in your 7th House (*see page 125*)

- Aquarius or Aquarius rising: it's in your 6th House (*see page 119*)

- Pisces or Pisces rising: it's in your 5th House (*see page 113*)

♌

The Upside of Mercury Retrograde in Leo

This is a time for playful creativity; let your ideas take their course, wherever they lead you. You can't control what's going on around you, so there's no point trying. This time can be quite restful and will allow you to fully focus on your creativity (instead of the applause!). For this reason, the retrograde can also be a very good time to go back to a creative project you worked on a while back but abandoned.

Romance issues are likely to hot up. Are you getting enough attention? Giving it? Does your beloved treat you like the queen or king you are? Are you confident enough in love? Love at the top of your agenda can be nice if your life is lacking romance, but the excess of passion can be a little tiring! In a good way, of course.

Now is also a good time to ask yourself if you have a tendency to show off, which does you no favours! That said, if you need confidence to shine in a particular situation, it's a good time to have another think about how you could fake it 'til you make it.

Five things to do

▶ Shine your light, if you were too shy to do so before.

▶ Be generous with someone you should have been generous with earlier.

▶ Direct your passion through artistic activity.

▶ Be open to new ideas and ways of having fun.

▶ Recommit to being more magnanimous and generous.

Watch out for...

The more power and responsibility you have, the more likely you are to lose your temper with people who aren't stepping up to the mark. And you might find your own aspirations are being put to the test. This isn't a good time to take risks. What looks good now could be dramatically disappointing in a few weeks' time, so tread with caution towards bright, shiny objects.

You can be so convinced of your brilliance that you find it hard to admit to your mistakes. Yes, your opinion's worth sharing, but it isn't the only opinion in town. It's also easy to fall into the trap of talking about what you'd like to do rather than actually doing it. And if you keep saying you're able to do anything, at some point you'll be put on the spot and have to prove it. Remember, you're not the only one who can be pushy and demanding.

How Mercury retrograde affects you

▶ Aries or Aries rising: it's in your 5th House (*see page 113*)

▶ Taurus or Taurus rising: it's in your 4th House (*see page 107*)

▶ Gemini or Gemini rising: it's in your 3rd House (*see page 101*)

▶ Cancer or Cancer rising: it's in your 2nd House (*see page 95*)

▶ Leo or Leo rising: it's in your 1st House (*see page 89*)

▶ Virgo or Virgo rising: it's in your 12th House (*see page 153*)

▶ Libra or Libra rising: it's in your 11th House (*see page 149*)

▶ Scorpio or Scorpio rising: it's in your 10th House (*see page 143*)

▶ Sagittarius or Sagittarius rising: it's in your 9th House (*see page 137*)

▶ Capricorn or Capricorn rising: it's in your 8th House (*see page 131*)

▶ Aquarius or Aquarius rising: it's in your 7th House (*see page 125*)

▶ Pisces or Pisces rising: it's in your 6th House (*see page 119*)

The Upside of Mercury Retrograde in Virgo

Virgo's diligence is something you can take advantage of during the Mercury retrograde. This is a great time for research and for redoing anything that isn't quite up to scratch. It's also a good time to get organized, file things away neatly and to clear clutter, especially in the workplace.

If you, or someone you care about, has a health concern, this is an excellent time to research both natural and conventional medical therapies.

If you need to quit any unhealthy habits, come up with a modest plan that you can realistically stick to and later build on, as needed.

Virgo is a sensual Earth sign, but it's also mercurial, so variety is welcome now. Tweak any area of your day-to-day life that could be improved by some extra spice or a fresh perspective.

Five things to do

▶ Double-check your work and finish anything you've half-started.

▶ Double-check any contracts you need to sign.

▶ Get rid of clutter.

▶ Get a health check-up.

▶ Revise your diet so it's healthier.

Watch out for...

There can be challenges in your workplace. Be prepared for delays and equipment breakdowns, as well as cranky co-workers. Double-checking all facts and figures is highly recommended at this time!

Although you need to think things through thoroughly under Mercury retrograde in Virgo, it's possible to go too far in your analysing and re-analysing: to the point where you end up letting opportunities pass you by while you're still making up your mind. Also, constant brooding can make you feel stressed. You need to relax from time to time or your health could suffer.

Here's something to think about under this cycle: there's only so far you can go when it comes to being helpful. Even though you may see solutions that aren't obvious to others, some people might interpret your offer of help as interfering. Similarly, you might feel resentful of anyone offering you help, feeling that you really know best. Instead of being fussy about everything being just so, choose your battles and don't be so hard on yourself. Also, try not to be picky about something from the past, unless you really feel it still needs 'fixing'.

How Mercury retrograde affects you

▶ Aries or Aries rising: it's in your 6th House (*see page 119*)

▶ Taurus or Taurus rising: it's in your 5th House (*see page 113*)

▶ Gemini or Gemini rising: it's in your 4th House (*see page 107*)

▶ Cancer or Cancer rising: it's in your 3rd House (*see page 101*)

▶ Leo or Leo rising: it's in your 2nd House (*see page 95*)

▶ Virgo or Virgo rising: it's in your 1st House (*see page 89*)

▶ Libra or Libra rising: it's in your 12th House (*see page 153*)

▶ Scorpio or Scorpio rising: it's in your 11th House (*see page 149*)

▶ Sagittarius or Sagittarius rising: it's in your 10th House (*see page 143*)

▶ Capricorn or Capricorn rising: it's in your 9th House (*see page 137*)

▶ Aquarius or Aquarius rising: it's in your 8th House (*see page 131*)

▶ Pisces or Pisces rising: it's in your 7th House (*see page 125*)

The Upside of Mercury Retrograde in Libra

The plus side of Mercury retrograde is definitely that old loves can come back into your life, if that's what you're pining for. This can be for reconciliation... or for closure. By the same token, if you really want to revive an old love affair, don't wait for a chance meeting. If Mercury is retrograde in Libra, the skies totally support you in getting back in touch. That said, there are no guarantees!

Libra is the sign most associated with fairness and justice. When Mercury is retrograde here, you may get a chance to right wrongs or perhaps get things done equitably to start with.

Also, old grievances and general relationship issues can come to the surface at this time, too. This can be positive, however, as it allows you to address problems you've been refusing to acknowledge and sort them out.

It's very likely going to be easier and more productive to have that difficult discussion, rather than avoid it. In fact, the discussion might not be necessary if you listen to what your loved one has to say. By resolving differences and mending ties, you can strengthen your relationships.

Five things to do

▶ Address old problems with your loved ones/be extra patient!

▶ Look up your ex or a friend or relative you fell out with and make peace.

▶ Forgive yourself for your past mistakes, especially those related to love or money.

▶ Renegotiate the terms of a personal or professional partnership.

▶ Nip relationship problems in the bud.

Watch out for...

A general sense that the world is out of balance leads to misunderstandings and communication going wrong – especially in close relationships. It might be a misinterpretation of a few words or a disagreement about a larger issue, but somehow you don't see eye to eye. A little patience can make all the difference.

Don't become heavily invested in decision-making. If you feel your input isn't being heard or valued, remember that the scales will likely dip in your favour before all the weighing is done.

Trying to keep the peace can push you into going along with whoever is around you – whether you think they are right or not – which can lead others to mistrust your judgement. Try to see things from their perspective and you'll find it much easier to make the right decisions.

People are likely to dither more than usual, including you, but perhaps some decisions don't need to be made immediately. If a relationship needs an overhaul, this is a great time for it. Tempting though it may be to go it alone, you'll feel much more fulfilled if you join forces with another.

How Mercury retrograde affects you

◗   If you're Aries or Aries rising: it's in your 7th House (*see page 125*)

◗   If you're Taurus or Taurus rising: it's in your 6th House (*see page 119*)

◗ If you're Gemini or Gemini rising: it's in your 5th House (*see page 113*)

◗ If you're Cancer or Cancer rising: it's in your 4th House (*see page 107*)

◗ If you're Leo or Leo rising: it's in your 3rd House (*see page 101*)

◗ If you're Virgo or Virgo rising: it's in your 2nd House (*see page 95*)

◗ If you're Libra or Libra rising: it's in your 1st House (*see page 89*)

◗ If you're Scorpio or Scorpio rising: it's in your 12th House (*see page 153*)

◗ If you're Sagittarius or Sagittarius rising: it's in your 11th House (*see page 149*)

◗ If you're Capricorn or Capricorn rising: it's in your 10th House (*see page 143*)

◗ If you're Aquarius or Aquarius rising: it's in your 9th House (*see page 137*)

◗ If you're Pisces or Pisces rising: it's in your 8th House (*see page 131*)

The Upside of Mercury Retrograde in Scorpio

It might not sound like the most fun thing to do with your time, but now is a time to face your inner demons and get them under control. Therapy for an issue from your past can go deeper now. Looking within rather than at the world around you is likely to be more productive.

More than any other sign, Scorpio likes to dig under the surface of things to see what's being glossed over or whitewashed. If there are secrets in your life, Mercury retrograde can work to shine a light on them. This may sound terrible, but it can actually be healing. That secret you've been trying to keep may not the big deal you once thought it was.

There's also a financial aspect here. It's the ideal time to renegotiate a financial partnership and/or pay off debts. Financial assets you've forgotten about or not even considered can resurface now. Something that seemed old and worn out, whether a friendship or a piece of clothing, can be transformed with very little effort.

Mercury in Scorpio is also a good time to work through a fear that has been holding you back. Doing that alone could change your life.

Five things to do

▶ Deal with old emotional baggage.

▶ Bring back sexy time.

▶ Explore your interest in arcane and esoteric matters.

▶ Focus on your debts and how you allocate your resources.

▶ Be open to your intuition and what it's telling you.

Watch out for...

It sounds OK in your head but saying mean or harsh words aloud can make you appear less than rational at this time. Perhaps it's because you feel more suspicious and insecure than usual. If so, now is the time to deal with those emotions. Talk to someone (preferably a professional) about where they came from.

Dishonesty of any kind is likely to come back to bite you when Mercury goes to and fro in Scorpio. Try to be honest with yourself and others while still being kind.

Try to avoid negative thinking, especially the impulse to lash out at someone before they can attack you. There are much better times to have a debate, so it makes sense to avoid contentious subjects at this time. That said, now is a good time for a deep and meaningful conversation you should have had earlier, if you can keep the conversation nice!

It's important at this time to be aware of the concept of sharing and all that it entails.

How Mercury retrograde affects you

▶ If you're Aries or Aries rising: it's in your 8th House (*see page 131*)

▶ If you're Taurus or Taurus rising: it's in your 7th House (*see page 125*)

▶ If you're Gemini or Gemini rising: it's in your 6th House (*see page 119*)

▶ If you're Cancer or Cancer rising: it's in your 5th House (*see page 113*)

- ❱ If you're Leo or Leo rising: it's in your 4th House (*see page 107*)

- ❱ If you're Virgo or Virgo rising: it's in your 3rd House (*see page 101*)

- ❱ If you're Libra or Libra rising: it's in your 2nd House (*see page 95*)

- ❱ If you're Scorpio or Scorpio rising: it's in your 1st House (*see page 89*)

- ❱ If you're Sagittarius or Sagittarius rising: it's in your 12th House (*see page 153*)

- ❱ If you're Capricorn or Capricorn rising: it's in your 11th House (*see page 149*)

- ❱ If you're Aquarius or Aquarius rising: it's in your 10th House (*see page 143*)

- ❱ If you're Pisces or Pisces rising: it's in your 9th House (*see page 137*)

♐

The Upside of Mercury Retrograde in Sagittarius

Here's your chance to look at the big picture of your life – again. If your plans have come unstuck recently, perhaps you've been focusing too much on the details? Upsets now can also simply be due to the fact that your timing was off.

Whatever is going on, use this time to realize there's a larger plan for you and to create a better, upgraded future.

It's also the ideal time to discipline yourself to step back and see how far you've come. Take another moment to re-count your blessings.

If you're lucky (and Sagittarius is a lucky sign) then you could find yourself retracing the fun of an old or previous adventure. If you're travelling abroad, it could be that you go back to somewhere you visited before – and hopefully have even more fun!

Five things to do

◗ Look to see how far you've come in life.

◗ Brush up on or start learning a foreign language.

◗ Investigate courses of study (but don't enrol until after the retrograde).

◗ Commit to a more optimistic outlook.

◗ Focus on the journey rather than the destination.

Watch out for...

This isn't an ideal time to travel if you can help it, unless you're returning somewhere. Be prepared to reschedule or reorganize your plans, go off your itinerary, or experience delays if you're on the move. If you can, it's possibly easier to stay local – otherwise, you'll need plenty of patience and a sense of humour. That said, if you're open to changes in your plans, you might even enjoy the journey.

There may be misunderstandings based on cultural clashes so it's important to develop greater sensitivity towards other people's feelings. Also, old legal matters can come up again and maybe even get sorted out.

Mercury retrograde in Sagittarius can stimulate opinions that would be better left unspoken. Although you probably have the right answers for you, they might not be right for anyone else. Not everything needs your input and saying nothing at all might be the wiser option, however difficult.

How Mercury retrograde affects you

◗ If you're Aries or Aries rising: it's in your 9th House (*see page 137*)

◗ If you're Taurus or Taurus rising: it's in your 8th House (*see page 131*)

◗ If you're Gemini or Gemini rising: it's in your 7th House (*see page 125*)

◗ If you're Cancer or Cancer rising: it's in your 6th House (*see page 119*)

◗ If you're Leo or Leo rising: it's in your 5th House (*see page 113*)

◗ If you're Virgo or Virgo rising: it's in your 4th House (*see page 107*)

◗ If you're Libra or Libra rising: it's in your 3rd House (*see page 101*)

▶ If you're Scorpio or Scorpio rising: it's in your 2nd House (*see page 95*)

▶ If you're Sagittarius or Sagittarius rising: it's in your 1st House (*see page 89*)

▶ If you're Capricorn or Capricorn rising: it's in your 12th House (*see page 153*)

▶ If you're Aquarius or Aquarius rising: it's in your 11th House (*see page 149*)

▶ If you're Pisces or Pisces rising: it's in your 10th House (*see page 143*)

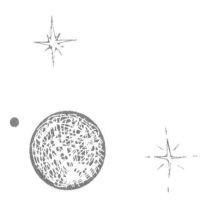

The Upside of Mercury Retrograde in Capricorn

During Mercury retrograde in Capricorn, we all start thinking more about how to achieve our goals. Perhaps you need to recommit to a goal or/and retrain? Now is the time to start planning. You can break down the steps to achieving your goal in a realistic way.

If you've been working hard on a project at work, this is the time to review it before you finish it. Yes, delays are possible now, but if you use the energies well, you could just give the whole thing one last good going over before submission. Potentially, this is also a very good time to take up again a work project you started earlier but let lapse.

Also, just for the record, because of the association that Capricorn has with tradition, this is also a great time to research your family history.

Five things to do

◗ Assess your career goals.

◗ Rebuild something, literally or metaphorically.

◗ Have a dental check-up but schedule dental work for after Mercury turns direct.

◗ Recommit to a life goal.

◗ Remember that there's more to life than work.

Watch out for...

It's not as if you're incapable of communicating – it's just that your words don't come out quite as kindly as the person you're speaking to might wish. What you consider being direct might be misconstrued as an accusation or command.

Try not to take on too many responsibilities. Your intentions are good, but if you're stage-managing others' lives, they aren't free to succeed or fail on their own terms. You aren't free to live your best life either.

This isn't the time to lay any kind of groundwork as there's a fair chance it will need to be redone. That said, it's a good time to re-lay groundwork.

Blind trust in authority could cause problems because it's hard to know which experts you can trust under this cycle. You might reconsider those you previously thought spoke with an air of wisdom. Your best guide is your own inner voice of authority.

How Mercury retrograde affects you

◗ If you're Aries or Aries rising: it's in your 10th House (*see page 143*)

◗ If you're Taurus or Taurus rising: it's in your 9th House (*see page 137*)

◗ If you're Gemini or Gemini rising: it's in your 8th House (*see page 131*)

◗ If you're Cancer or Cancer rising: it's in your 7th House (*see page 125*)

◗ If you're Leo or Leo rising: it's in your 6th House (*see page 119*)

◗ If you're Virgo or Virgo rising: it's in your 5th House (*see page 113*)

◗ If you're Libra or Libra rising: it's in your 4th House (*see page 107*)

▶ If you're Scorpio or Scorpio rising: it's in your 3rd House (*see page 101*)

▶ If you're Sagittarius or Sagittarius rising: it's in your 2nd House (*see page 95*)

▶ If you're Capricorn or Capricorn rising: it's in your 1st House (*see page 89*)

▶ If you're Aquarius or Aquarius rising: it's in your 12th House (*see page 153*)

▶ If you're Pisces or Pisces rising: it's in your 11th House (*see page 149*)

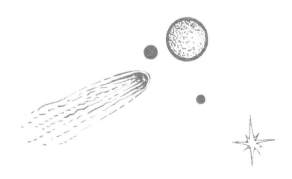

The Upside of Mercury Retrograde in Aquarius

This is a great time for intellectual growth. You can throw out any outmoded ideas based on what you think is right and replace them with real facts by looking into matters more deeply and asking questions.

You feel creative and ideas flow thick and fast. Your final decisions should wait but you can begin to re-evaluate everything.

Aquarius has a very charitable side to it, so if you had plans to do something for humanity that got shelved because life got too busy, this is a great time to take up that plan again.

It's also a time when you can be more mentally detached – a good thing in science and finances, among other things, but less good for dealing with loving relationships.

Five things to do

◗ Decide whether any group or society you belong to still suits your needs.

◗ Check your computer for viruses and malware.

◗ Review your dearest wishes – do you still want what you used to want?

◗ Look up an old friend you haven't seen for years.

◗ Get back to your astrological studies.

Watch out for...

Old friends may re-enter your life but you'll need to re-assess what friendship actually means to you. It might be that someone close to you lets you down or doesn't act as you expected. Beware of squabbles, misunderstandings and miscommunications among your friends. Committing to talking things through (again) with friends is a key to making the most of Mercury retrograde in Aquarius.

Mercury retrograde in Aquarius can put your thoughts in a feedback loop or echo chamber and your thinking can be especially affected by confirmation bias. It's harder – but therefore more important – to be objective and appreciate the value of other perspectives.

Frustrations with technology are more likely now because Aquarius is associated with tech. Computers seem out to get you, eating files and directing your emails to the wrong person. If in any doubt, get someone to check your gadgets are working properly.

Change is constant, so it's wise not to argue out of pride or attachment to how things were yesterday. To change the world, you need to change your own mind.

How Mercury retrograde affects you

▶ If you're Aries or Aries rising: it's in your 11th House (*see page 149*)

▶ If you're Taurus or Taurus rising: it's in your 10th House (*see page 143*)

▶ If you're Gemini or Gemini rising: it's in your 9th House (*see page 137*)

▶ If you're Cancer or Cancer rising: it's in your 8th House (*see page 131*)

▶ If you're Leo or Leo rising: it's in your 7th House (*see page 125*)

▶ If you're Virgo or Virgo rising: it's in your 6th House (*see page 119*)

▶ If you're Libra or Libra rising: it's in your 5th House (*see page 113*)

▶ If you're Scorpio or Scorpio rising: it's in your 4th House (*see page 107*)

▶ If you're Sagittarius or Sagittarius rising: it's in your 3rd House (*see page 101*)

▶ If you're Capricorn or Capricorn rising: it's in your 2nd House (*see page 95*)

▶ If you're Aquarius or Aquarius rising: it's in your 1st House (*see page 89*)

▶ If you're Pisces or Pisces rising: it's in your 12th House (*see page 153*)

♓

The Upside of Mercury Retrograde in Pisces

On the one hand, this is a positive because Mercury is the planet of the mind and where Mercury goes, our minds follow. Under Mercury retrograde in the dreamy and spiritual sign of Pisces, we have a longer time to focus on the mystical. That said, Pisces is already a potentially foggy sign, so Mercury retrograde can up the confusion!

Spending your time on hobbies that don't involve your rational mind – such as gardening, painting or music – will bring the mental space you need now to allow you to bring clarity to your feelings. Artistic skills are heightened under this cycle, and it's a very good time to revisit any projects you've left incomplete.

If you had a dream that you abandoned, allow yourself some time with it again – especially any creative projects with a mystical or musical bent.

Five things to do

▶ Take up meditation again, if you've stopped.

▶ Listen to music that you loved years ago.

▶ Re-think your boundaries.

▶ Rediscover your kind and compassionate side.

▶ Re-read favourite books or re-watch favourite films; or just get lost in daydreams.

Watch out for...

With your brain being so fuddled, it's easy for smooth talkers to persuade you into buying whatever they're selling. Just accept you're likely to be gullible and delay purchase until later, when you can think more clearly.

When your thoughts are redirected to Piscean realms, it may be difficult to tell fact from fiction. Believing our judgement is infallible makes us vulnerable to delusion, so remember that things are not always as they seem, then try to relax and enjoy the show.

Pisces has an association with unhealthy, even addictive, behaviours as a way of escaping the pressures or boredom of daily life. Consider making positive changes that will feed your imagination and soul.

Feeling so dreamy means you may stare into space for hours on end. Conversations drift into strange territory and your memory is completely unreliable. You might be tempted to run away and hide from the world – it's worth obeying that feeling, just temporarily.

How Mercury retrograde affects you

▶ If you're Aries or Aries rising: it's in your 12th House (*see page 153*)

▶ If you're Taurus or Taurus rising: it's in your 11th House (*see page 149*)

▶ If you're Gemini or Gemini rising: it's in your 10th House (*see page 143*)

▶ If you're Cancer or Cancer rising: it's in your 9th House (*see page 137*)

▶ If you're Leo or Leo rising: it's in your 8th House (*see page 131*)

▶ If you're Virgo or Virgo rising: it's in your 7th House (*see page 125*)

▶ If you're Libra or Libra rising: it's in your 6th House (*see page 119*)

● If you're Scorpio or Scorpio rising: it's in your
5th House (*see page 113*)

● If you're Sagittarius or Sagittarius rising: it's in your
4th House (*see page 107*)

● If you're Capricorn or Capricorn rising: it's in your
3rd House (*see page 101*)

● If you're Aquarius or Aquarius rising: it's in your
2nd House (*see page 95*)

● If you're Pisces or Pisces rising: it's in your 1st House
(*see page 89*)

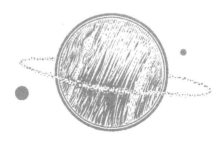

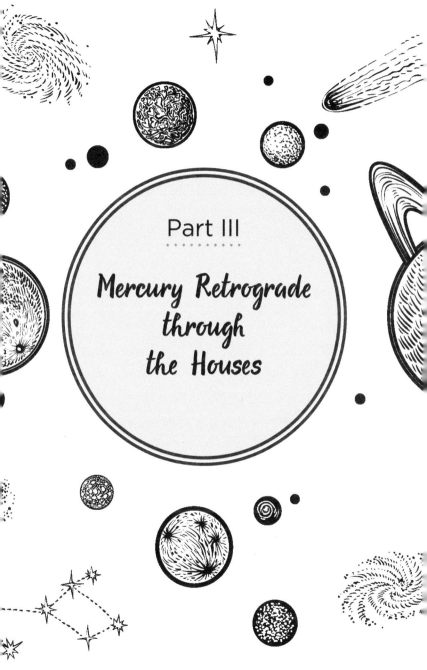

Part III

Mercury Retrograde through the Houses

The sign in which Mercury is retrograde affects *how* it manifests its energies. However, if you want to know what it means for you specifically, you need to know which House it falls in, in your chart. The House describes the area of your life in which the retrograde has the strongest effect. It might seem complicated but it's really worth delving into for the insights it brings!

If you've had your birth chart calculated, you can look at your chart to see which House Mercury retrograde falls in. Alternatively, you can look at the House in relation to your Star sign or Rising sign. (Visit www.theastrologybook. com/freechart to find your Rising sign.) Knowing your Rising sign will give you a *much* more accurate reading.

Why it's important to know your Rising sign

With the advent of technology, more and more people know their Rising sign, and it's important in understanding the impact of Mercury retrograde on you because:

▶ Your Star sign (called your Sun sign by astrologers) is interesting but it's only used in horoscopes because most people know it – it's easy. The Sun moves through the 12 signs of the zodiac at around the same time each year (give or take). So, most people know if they were born, say, on 14 April they're an Aries or 1 September, they're a Virgo, or 8 November, they're a Scorpio. But most people don't know their Rising sign. This is why, traditionally, most people only ever read their Star sign.

▶ Your Rising sign, however, is the most personal point in your chart and, moreover, it's the gateway to your chart. There are 12 sections (aka Houses) in your chart and they all follow on from the Rising sign. This is a bit complicated to understand without at least a full day's astrology training, so please believe us when we say the Rising sign is important.

▶ If you read your Star sign, you'll get a quick fix of information. If you read your Rising sign as well, it will actually be more like getting a personal one-on-one reading with an astrologer and you'll get a far more accurate reading.

The first thing to do is use the tables in the Appendix (*see pages 179–182*) to discover the sign in which Mercury is retrograde. Then read the information in Part II to discover what that means, and in which House in your chart the cycle is taking place, based on your Star sign or Rising sign. (Remember, reading your Rising sign will give you a more accurate description of what to expect.)

About the cosmic extras

The House occupied by the Mercury retrograde offers those on a spiritual path a chance to connect more deeply to the energies of the retrograde cycle – perhaps by using affirmations, a particular essential oil or working with a particular goddess or archangel.

Working with the cosmic extras in this section is a simple and practical way to tune in in a more positive way. To make the most of this time and to hear any of the messages the Universe is trying to send you, we suggest that you:

◗ Repeat the given affirmations throughout the cycle.

◗ Use the oil mentioned in a diffuser or add a few drops to your bath.

◗ Invoke the archangel and/or goddess. You could do this by printing out an image of them from the Internet and putting it up on your home altar or setting it as your phone lock screen or computer desktop. Just talk to the deity about whatever you're going through and ask them for help and guidance on your journey.

Mercury Retrograde in Your 1st House

There could be confusion about your image, your reputation and how others see you during this cycle. It may also be the time to make some important, if superficial, changes. For example, now is a good time to rethink your image. Even if you're happy with who you are, you might want to ask yourself if you're getting your message across to others. Perhaps it's time to think about a revamp?

When Mercury is retrograde here, ask if you're still wearing the same protective mask or persona that you did when you were a child. If so, does it still fit or should you update your presentation?

Mercury retrograde in your sign can also be a time when life seems to hit one snag after another. Others find it harder than usual to understand what you're trying to say to them, and you'll find it impossible to write anything without at least one grammatical or spelling mistake per line. This is a small price to pay for a period when you get to re-evaluate your old life, the chance to decide whether you're happy with what you've left behind and where you're going.

In a nutshell

This is a super intense Mercury retrograde cycle because your 1st House is such a personal part of your chart and all about how you come across in the world. When Mercury is retrograde here, it's very much a time to think about the image you present to the world – and make changes to it if necessary.

Five things to do

◗   Take extra time when making decisions.

◗   Re-evaluate your image and make changes if you think they're necessary.

◗   Make a list of what you want to accomplish.

◗   Slow down, think first, speak after.

◗   Revamp your business cards/website/anything that presents you to the world.

The upside

You can totally change your image during this cycle – or at least decide how you want to change. However, it's probably not a good idea to drastically cut your hair or donate most your existing wardrobe to charity until after the retrograde. This really is a cycle where you can make big life changes, in particular doing something that you know you should have done earlier.

Watch out for...

You may find yourself tripping over words or unable to express yourself in a way you'd like. Hasty words can do a lot of damage; it's not only what you say: watch your body language too as you may be giving off mixed signals.

Is there really any point having the same old arguments again and again? Although you do get a second shot at getting things right, constantly going over old ground will just wear you down to a frazzle.

Be careful not to judge too quickly – you may not have all the facts at your disposal yet. Or you might not truly understand what's going on. It might test your temper and patience but holding back a while will make life much easier in the long run.

Cosmic extras

Top three affirmations: These affirmations are designed to help you make the most of Mercury retrograde in your 1st House. Choose one and repeat it all day, then choose another and repeat that, then choose the third and go with that. Repeat often.

I am a work in progress!

Patience is a virtue.

I look before I leap.

Essential oil: Angelica

Goddess: Athena, the warrior goddess and protector

Archangel: Ariel, the outdoorsy angel

After the retrograde

After the retrograde, Mercury resumes normal communication transmission and moves forwards again, meaning things should be less complicated from here on in – for a while at least. If Mercury was retrograding in your 1st House, your entire life has potentially been subject to madness and mayhem as Mercury played his funny tricks all over you. If life has been chaotic beyond belief of late, Mercury was very likely the cause. As Mercury changes direction you can expect (or at least allow for the possibility of) one last blast of mayhem. After that, it's smoother sailing. There will be fewer crossed wires, less drama and much, much less to-ing and fro-ing.

Mercury Retrograde in Your 2nd House

You can expect to be doing some rethinking and reconsidering about cash, property and/or your possessions during this cycle. Your self-esteem and what you really value is also up for a rethink.

It may also be time to reconsider what's important to you in life. It sounds like a big question and, yes, it is. But you only get the occasional chance to really revise such major issues. So, what really matters to you? Is your current lifestyle supporting what you believe to be important in the great scheme of things? If you've been feeling negative about yourself lately, this cycle asks you to think again about your opinion of yourself! Rate yourself more highly and more money will follow. It's the law of attraction. Also, what good does it do you to act small?

The 2nd House is about cash, property and possessions, so you do need to be extra careful when making financial transactions because there's extra room for confusion. That said, most positively, it's a very good time to rethink your finances, and money owed to you could finally turn up. If you're trying to make a big decision regarding buying or selling property, gather the facts first.

In a nutshell

Expect the opportunity to do something again, especially when it comes to money, banking, PayPal, cryptocurrency or anything else to do with cash, property or possessions. This is an awesome cycle, not least because it has so much to teach us about the energetic connections between self-esteem and money. Money is energy, remember, so it's a good time to rethink your attitudes to cash. Do you think you're worthy of the money you'd like to earn? That's the key.

Five things to do

◗ Look for new ways to make money, based on your talents and values.

◗ Ask if you need to repair, revamp, replace or donate any of your possessions.

◗ Pay overdue bills, after checking for any errors.

◗ Open a savings or retirement account.

◗ Make a list of what you value most and change your ways accordingly.

The upside

So, overall, this is an excellent time to revisit old, nagging issues in terms of your finances. Perhaps there's a better bank account to switch to or a credit card with a lower interest rate. Or maybe you could pay your bills on a different, more convenient, day of the month. Spending a little time reviewing how you handle your money could save you a small fortune in the long run.

If you get really lucky during this cycle, it could be that you finally receive cash you earned earlier (perhaps even under a previous retrograde cycle).

Watch out for...

You need to keep a really close eye on your finances under this cycle – including what you thought you'd already sorted out. Money due in might just as easily be delayed; you could have an unexpected expense come up, or you could overlook something in your budget or miscalculate. What's for sure is that Mercury retrograde in your 2nd House potentially plays havoc with your cash flow. It helps if you put a little aside in advance.

If you feel less confident and a little unsure of yourself under this cycle, maybe you've been clinging onto things you no longer need. Things that no longer support who you are today. If something doesn't make you feel safe, secure and happy, it may be time to replace it with something else or just let it go.

Cosmic extras

Top three affirmations: These affirmations are designed to help you make the most of Mercury retrograde in your 2nd House. Choose one and repeat it all day, then choose another and repeat that, then choose the third and go with that. Repeat often.

Now is the time to review my financial plans.

Money owed to me flows to me now.

I am worth more than I think I am.

Essential oil: Ylang ylang

Goddess: Abundantia, goddess of abundance

Archangel: Chamuel, the angel of love

After the retrograde

After the retrograde, Mercury resumes normal transmission and goes forwards again, which means some of the financial confusion should be about to ease up. Mercury has been retrograde in your 2nd House of cash, property and possessions. If you've been going two steps forwards and one step back where any or all of those subjects are concerned, you can thank Mercury! As Mercury changes direction, expect (allow for) one last blast of financial mayhem. And after that? Your finances should start to make more sense, there will be fewer annoying glitches when it comes to dealing with money, and if you're trying to buy or sell something, you can expect a lot less weirdness.

Mercury Retrograde in Your 3rd House

Mercury is now retrograde in the part of your chart connected to communication, your brothers and sisters, your neighbourhood and quick trips. When Mercury appears to go backwards here you can expect to have to do some rethinking and reconsidering on one of these subjects – for example, sorting things out with a sibling or taking back something you said. There could also be confusion in one of these areas, so don't panic. If you haven't backed up your computer files or your digital photos in a while, this is an ideal time to do it. Remember, Mercury is the trickster of the zodiac, so if you do back them up, chances are you won't lose them – but if you don't...

This cycle is actually strong for you as you have the planet of communications retrograde in your House of communications – it's what you'd call a double whammy. Missed phone calls, lost phones, emails and texts accidentally sent to the wrong person and botched travel plans and rendezvous are possible. But there's also the chance to rethink a very important issue in your life. If you're signing an agreement, be *sure* both parties are on the same page.

In a nutshell

This is the House you reason from – and when Mercury is retrograde here, you can change your mind. But most importantly, it's the part of your chart where you connect with others and talk to them or exchange with them. So, Mercury retrograde here opens the way to mixed-up communications but also to getting back in touch with people you've lost contact with.

Five things to do

▶ Back up your computer (also check it for viruses and malware).

▶ Reconnect with your siblings.

▶ Get your car serviced – but get a guarantee in case any problem recurs.

▶ Charge your mobile regularly.

▶ Keep a diary – it's all too easy to forget appointments.

The upside

This is also a good time to pick up old writing projects, have a conversation over again or arrange a get together with siblings or neighbours. If there are any outstanding issues between you, now is the time to get them sorted out.

You might notice things in your environment you never saw before, which will give you added insight into what you should do next.

Mercury retrograde here can also give you a chance to say something you wished you'd said earlier – in particular, it can work well if you meant to say something kind but missed your chance.

Watch out for...

Communication really can be very frustrating – other scenarios include your phone running out of power, accidentally hitting Reply All, and just general misunderstandings galore. Make sure you've understood the other person's point of view before you go off the deep end. And don't make promises you can't keep.

Mercury retrograde here also affects all short journeys and forms of transport. If you drive, watch the speed limit and don't park where you shouldn't. The chances of getting a ticket now are much higher than usual. Check your oil and water before a long drive and *make sure you've got plenty of fuel*. If you rely on public transport, be prepared for delays and cancellations.

Technology seems to hate you just now. Don't fret – it isn't personal. Take a deep breath and try again when something doesn't work. Although it *might* have broken down, there's also a fair chance you're the one to blame. It doesn't matter how often and how hard you press the button if it's the wrong button.

Cosmic extras

Top three affirmations: These affirmations are designed to help you make the most of Mercury retrograde in your 3rd House. Choose one and repeat it all day, then choose another and repeat that, then choose the third and go with that. Repeat often.

I am OK to talk things through again and again.

It's never too late to say sorry.

I am patient and I believe in second chances.

Essential oil: Bergamot

Goddess: Saraswati, goddess of wisdom

Archangel: Zadkiel, angel of compassion

After the retrograde

Mercury going forwards again in this part of your chart will help you think better. Mercury has been retrograde in your 3rd House of communications, neighbours and siblings – so it's likely you've been having issues in at least one of those areas. As Mercury changes direction, there could be one last twist and then life should settle down. Getting your message through to people will be easier. You'll receive fewer mixed messages. Upsets with neighbours and siblings can be resolved. Overall, life will be easier to handle in every way.

Mercury Retrograde in Your 4th House

Nothing is set in stone regarding your family or your home as Mercury 'goes backwards' through your 4th House. There could be confusion on the domestic front, or delays, or you could find something from your past being dug up somehow. For example, someone important from your past could come up in conversation, and suddenly you find yourself up to date with their news, whether you wanted to be or not. Or perhaps you're clearing up your home (or renovating or moving) and you find some item from your past that takes you down memory lane.

Family issues from the past can come up again and even be solved now. If you're not happy with the way your home is organized, now is an ideal time to redo it. For some, there will be big confusion about whether to stay or leave their current home, and others will have the chance to revisit a place they used to call home. Don't feel pressured into making decisions.

In a nutshell

This is the part of the chart that's all about home and family; it's about where you feel you belong and the people who feel like family to you. So, when Mercury is retrograde here, these parts of life can be 'hit' (ideally, they will be worked on for longer than usual and sorted out). If there are family upsets and rifts to be healed, you can look to this cycle to fix them.

Five things to do

◗ Reconnect with your family.

◗ Redecorate or do repairs around your home.

◗ Research your family history.

◗ Get any deals related to your home in writing or risk having to negotiate them again.

◗ Make peace with your past.

The upside

Although you might think about moving at this time, it's best to avoid making a hasty decision and research your options instead. The same goes for major home improvements, though small ones can work just fine, especially if you did the last round under a previous Mercury retrograde.

On the contrary, this is a good time for making plans to do with home and family. If you feel stuck in a rut, maybe the energy in your home is also stuck. Changing your furniture around can give you a whole new perspective.

This is also a very good time to go 'back home' and/or revisit the past. This House denotes the womb and is the 'cellar' of your chart – it's about the past and what you've stashed away, down in the cellar of your life (which is why family is also here – the people with whom you shared your past and those who helped shape you).

It's about instinct and where you feel safe. Parents in general, and the father specifically, are also represented here. Again, Mercury retrograde here gives you more time to rethink, review and maybe even reconnect with anyone or anything to do with the 4th House.

Watch out for...

All sorts of minor domestic problems can arise. Chances are, they aren't new – they're just brought more sharply into focus. A slight drip now can lead to a major flood later, so it's time to tackle all those little repair jobs around the house.

A family member might bring up an issue from the past that you thought was well and truly dead and buried. You're older and wiser now, and there might be enough new information, so your perspective is totally different. If you're unlucky though, they might just be harping on about the same old thing. Be as non-judgemental as you can. Your negativity might be habitual if the issue dates from way back. Try to look at the issue afresh.

Cosmic extras

Top three affirmations: These affirmations are designed to help you make the most of Mercury retrograde in your 4th House. Choose one and repeat it all day, then choose another and repeat that, then choose the third and go with that. Repeat often.

> *Upsets with family/roommates are*
> *opportunities to clear the air.*
>
> *It's only when you look back that*
> *you see how far you've come.*
>
> *Now is the time for me to reorganize my home.*

Essential oil: Patchouli

Goddess: Diana, goddess of witches

Archangel: Gabriel, the family angel

After the retrograde

Mercury has been retrograde in your 4th House, so home, family and domestic matters have been the focus. For some this has been about going back to somewhere they used to call home. For others, life at home has been chaotic beyond belief, and this is almost certainly why!

Misunderstandings with your live-in lover, spouse or roommates should ease up once the retrograde is done. Even your parents will start to understand you better. As Mercury actually changes direction, expect one last blast of mayhem. And after that? Your home life and family will still take up a lot of your headspace but there will be a lot less confusion and upset.

Mercury Retrograde in Your 5th House

When Mercury is retrograde in your 5th House, you get a chance to have a rethink about situations involving children, creativity and light-hearted romance, so don't panic if you're currently experiencing delays or confusion connected to one or all of these subjects. For example, if your partner wants a child and you're not so sure, or vice versa, this is the time the subject could come up. Or maybe one of you has children from a previous relationship and there are issues to deal with. Or maybe you're rethinking an entire romance. It's a good time to do that!

Creatively, it could be you're working on something and you're not sure whether to redo it or scrap it and just start over. Wait before you decide. In other cases, you and your partner seem to be missing each other's mark.

In a nutshell

This is the House of romance, creativity and kids – the fun zone of your chart. It's your downtime. It's your light-hearted side and what you do on the weekend. It's where you express yourself and even take some personal risks. It's the House of flirtation and good times. So, when Mercury is retrograde here, any and all of these parts of your life can be a bit befuddled.

Five things to do

◗ Get back to an old hobby.

◗ Indulge your inner child and play a game.

◗ Spend more time with children.

◗ Relight the fire with your current lover.

◗ Brush up on your flirting technique.

The upside

You might be so busy that having fun seems unlikely, so make the time for it. You're probably more popular than usual and can pick and choose from invitations.

You might also hear from a past love. It might not be a bad idea to reconnect, but keep in mind there's a reason why they're in your past. You can finally see how far you've come. There's also the possibility of injecting some romance back into a jaded relationship.

You may see different ways to express your creative self. This is a great time for exploring the fun-loving parts of yourself.

Watch out for...

It can feel as if there's a lack of creative energy. Perhaps your confidence has been dented. Remember, you don't need to compare yourself to others and some projects take time to ferment. Try to avoid rushing things. There's possibly less of a spark around the things you usually love. Try to be less judgemental and slow down a bit.

It's an interesting time to start a new love affair. If you do meet someone new, things may change after Mercury goes direct, so take things easy at the start. Things are extra likely to go wrong with dates – calls might not be returned or perhaps other people will be late or cancel.

Arguments with a loved one could be blown out of all proportion. It could be that it's all over and an unmitigated disaster, but maybe, just maybe, you're being a teensy bit overdramatic.

Cosmic extras

Top three affirmations: These affirmations are designed to help you make the most of Mercury retrograde in your 5th House. Choose one and repeat it all day, then choose another and repeat that, then choose the third and go with that. Repeat often.

I am reconnecting with my inner child.

Old ways of having fun are new again.

I am re-exploring my creative side.

Essential oil: Cinnamon

Goddess: Medusa, the Sun goddess

Archangel: Raziel, the esoteric teacher

After the retrograde

If you've had endless queries about life, romance, kids and creativity, here's why: Mercury has been retrograde in your 5th House of children, creativity and romance. If you've been going two steps forwards and one step back where any or all of those subjects are concerned, this is the cosmic reason. As Mercury changes direction, you can expect one last bit of confusion around these subjects. But after that, you should start to understand what it was all about.

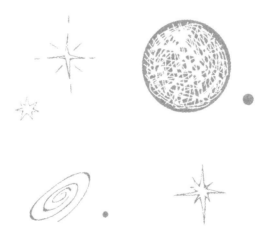

Mercury Retrograde in Your 6th House

Expect to be rethinking and reconsidering your daily work and health routines. There could also be confusion in one of these areas. If you find an old health concern comes back at this time, try not to be alarmed and instead look at it as a chance to release the malady forever. There are times when Mercury retrograde means we can somehow put an end to something that started under a previous Mercury retrograde. So, if you have a health problem that first emerged while this planet was in 'reverse', you may find the coming few weeks give you the chance to knock it on the head.

This cycle is also good if you've been slacking off when it comes to your fitness routines. Get back into them now and you shouldn't have to wrestle too hard to keep it all up until at least the next Mercury cycle. At work, this period gives you the chance to renegotiate your daily duties. Think about what you'd like to change.

In a nutshell

The 6th House is where we do our daily grind and earn our daily bread. It's where we do things for other people and perform our work duties. It's the 'ticking over' part of your horoscope – not the most glamorous part, but very useful and practical. It reveals how well you do or don't look after yourself. If your inner physician is handy with a poultice, tincture or some Reiki, so much the better. Pets are also found in this House. And when Mercury is retrograde here, all of this is up for a rethink.

Five things to do

◗   Change to a healthier diet.

◗   Rethink your morning and evening routines.

◗   Recommit to exercise.

◗   Take yourself and/or your pet for a check-up.

◗   Rebuild relationships with workmates.

The upside

You're definitely being summoned to review the way you take care of your body. Maybe you need a healthier diet or to increase or change the exercise you do (assuming you do any!)

You can begin by making a list of what you're eating now so you can see where changes are needed.

This is also a good time to reorganize your workspace, office or desk. In fact, anything to do with your daily working life is up for review now. If you feel like your routines aren't working for you, this is the time to do something about it.

Watch out for...

It might feel as if your schedule has been thrown out of the window. Although routines give your life a structure, they can also be dull and predictable. A little flexibility helps.

It's a good idea to make sure your health check-ups are up to date. Old health problems can resurface, but tests performed now may be inconclusive. It's better to research the possibilities and act once Mercury is direct again.

Problems at work are possible. You might clash with co-workers, miss deadlines or find you've got things wrong somehow and have to redo work. There's no harm in rethinking the suitability of your job but avoid making any premature decisions. However bad it gets, remind yourself it's only temporary. Don't dramatically walk out of your job just now – even if that's the right option in the long term.

Cosmic extras

Top three affirmations: These affirmations are designed to help you make the most of Mercury retrograde in your 6th House. Choose one and repeat it all day, then choose another and repeat that, then choose the third and go with that. Repeat often.

*I am rethinking my daily morning
and evening routines.*

I am getting back into a systematic health regime.

*I am reorganizing my duties and
considering how I am of service.*

Essential oil: Tea tree

Goddess: Ceres, the fertility goddess

Archangel: Metatron, the energy clearer

After the retrograde

The end of the retrograde is great news for you if daily life has had you on the hop. Mercury has been retrograde in your 6th House, so you may have felt as though you've been going two steps forwards and one step back in your daily life and where a health matter is concerned. If, on the other hand, you've used the past few weeks to redirect your daily duties or to get back into health routines you'd allowed to lapse, good for you – you've made the most of the cycle. As Mercury changes direction there could be a bit more weirdness, but then you should expect a lot less uncertainty in your daily life.

Mercury Retrograde in Your 7th House

Your 7th House is the part of your chart that's connected to your most important personal relationships – past, present or potential. A word of warning, though: it's also the part of your chart related to your open enemies. When Mercury 'goes backwards' here you can expect to be rethinking and reconsidering your love life – and there could well be confusion in one of these areas. For some, the most obvious manifestation of this cycle will be the reappearance of an ex. Yes, it might be a chance to get back together, but it can also provide you with another opportunity – the chance to better understand why you split before you move on.

New couples should take care now not to let minor misunderstandings get in the way of a blossoming romance. All couples should remember that missed connections, confused conversations and lost emails and text messages are more likely, and act accordingly.

In a nutshell

This is the House where you find the Descendant (or 'love line'). It's about the 'other' – the important other people in your life. That could be your beloved, your ex or even people who are more like foes than friends but who loom large in your life. It can also be best friends, business partners and bosses – anyone who is a VIP in your life. So, of course, Mercury retrograde here throws a bit of mayhem and confusion on relationships of all kinds. It also tends to bring exes out of the woodwork.

Five things to do

◗ Bury the hatchet with an enemy or frenemy.

◗ Contact an old friend you haven't spoken to lately.

◗ Renegotiate the terms of a partnership.

◗ Reconcile with an ex (or get closure).

◗ Work to achieve balance in your relationships.

The upside

In business, this is a good time to find new customers because they will buy from you again and are more likely to refer others to you.

If you need to reconnect with an old partner, reconcile with an enemy or recommit to something, this is an excellent time to do so.

If you split up from someone a while ago (especially if it was under a previous Mercury retrograde cycle) this can be a good time to get back in touch, be it for reconciliation or closure. You may find they simply 'turn up' in your life.

Watch out for...

You may need to renegotiate the terms of your closest relationship. There are often unspoken agreements that have developed over time and simply been accepted. But now it's time to address these unspoken agreements and decide whether they're really what you want.

Alternatively, old issues that you thought were done and dusted might arise again and you might have to bite your tongue. Sometimes it can be good to air differences of opinion and it can deepen your understanding of each other. As communication problems are likely, beware of misunderstandings.

A new relationship that starts when Mercury is retrograde in your 7th House might turn out to be a bit confusing or on-again/off-again.

Traditionally this isn't an ideal time to sign any sort of contract, including a marriage contract, mainly because of potential SNAFUs. See an astrologer if you're worried. Mercury retrograde unions can and do last! If you really have to sign a contract, make sure you check the small print first.

Cosmic extras

Top three affirmations: These affirmations are designed to help you make the most of Mercury retrograde in your 7th House. Choose one and repeat it all day, then choose another and repeat that, then choose the third and go with that. Repeat often.

The loves of my past create my love life today – where to next?

I love myself enough to talk any upsets through with anyone.

I will always connect with the people I love, and they with me.

Essential oil: Jasmine

Goddess: Lakshmi, goddess of love, wealth and beauty

Archangel: Jophiel, the angel of beauty

After the retrograde

Mercury going forwards again could impact your love life, since Mercury has been retrograde in your 7th House of relationships, aka your 'love zone'. If you've been feeling like your love life is going slightly crazy – for example, if you and your partner have been missing each other's calls and are having one misunderstanding after another or you just haven't been able to connect – you now know the cause is Mercury retrograde. As Mercury changes direction, there could be a tad more strangeness and then your love life will start to make more sense. You can expect a lot less confusion and romantic madness.

Mercury Retrograde in Your 8th House

It's time to have another think about who you're 'getting into bed with', both financially and sexually! When Mercury is retrograde in your 8th House, anything related to joint financial ventures, sex and intimacy is up for debate. Joint finances refer to your salary, credit cards and loans – wherever your money is tied up with someone else's. It can also be where it's tied up with a partner, past or present. When Mercury 'goes backwards' in this part of your chart, you can expect to be rethinking or reconsidering one of these subjects. If you have a history of attracting the 'wrong' type of partner, ask yourself why that might be. Are you attracted to people with qualities that you don't want to acknowledge in yourself?

There could also be confusion in one of these areas, so look at how well you're relating to people on an intimate level. If you're keeping people at arms' length (whether by being stand-offish or by constantly cracking jokes, for example), now is the time for you to do some serious thinking about the barriers you're putting up.

This part of your chart is also about jealousy and obsession. For some, an old jealousy problem will come back – see if you can deal better with it this time around. For others, if you tend to try to control other people, now is the time to (a) deal with the fallout from that and (b) work out a better way to carry yourself.

In a nutshell

The 8th House rules sex and joint finances. For some, this is a sinister House – if you go through ancient astrological manuscripts you'll find all manner of strange writings about death. The 8th House was once the House of death, but these days we think of it in more enlightened terms – the House of death and rebirth, for instance. That brings a sort of Buddhist feeling into this otherwise slightly frightening domain. Think of this House as the phoenix rising from the ashes or the leaves that wither and disappear into the soil, only to be reabsorbed and later brought back to life when another plant flourishes there.

Five things to do

▶ Call in debts.

▶ Renew your insurance.

▶ Avoid relying on other people's money or money owed to you.

▶ Review your loans and see if you can get a better deal.

▶ Get rid of something you've been planning to.

The upside

If people owe you money, try sending out some invoice reminders. This is an excellent time to get money returned. It's also a good time to renew your insurance policies and pay your tax bill.

If you're working on a financial plan, it's a great time to give it another once-over. Sure, it can be a confusing time but the advantage of having Mercury retrograde in your 8th House is that you actually have more time to work out how to sort out any financial questions.

As there's also a sexual element to this House, it can be a time when an old flame returns for some classic 'sex with an ex'. Enjoy – if you think it's a good idea!

Watch out for...

This retrograde affects the resources you receive from others, and promises may be broken or delayed. Pay special attention to loans and debts as you might be charged wrongly.

You might have to discuss sexual issues, and intimacy can be harder to achieve. This can partly be due to secrets coming to light at this time. Feeling overly emotional and pessimistic can make you see the worst in every situation. If you can't deal with matters with sensitivity, and be positive, it might be best to wait until Mercury is direct again before having any big discussions.

Cosmic extras

Top three affirmations: These affirmations are designed to help you make the most of Mercury retrograde in your 8th House. Choose one and repeat it all day, then choose another and repeat that, then choose the third and go with that. Repeat often.

I am taken care of materially.

All my financial needs are being met.

My sex life is wonderfully healthy.

Essential oil: Myrrh

Goddess: Kali, who liberates us

Archangel: Jeremiel, the life reviewer

After the retrograde

Mercury going forwards again in this part of your chart should be good news. For weeks, there have likely been stalls and queries to do with sex and money. Now it's time to analyse the facts. As Mercury has been retrograde in your 8th House of shared finances (credit cards, loans, salary, etc.) and sex, you've probably been dealing with issues to do with sex and joint financial ventures. As Mercury changes direction, expect a bit more confusion and then your finances and sex life will start to make more sense – and you should find there are fewer misunderstandings with your partner.

Mercury Retrograde in Your 9th House

This is the part of your chart connected to your 'cosmic path' through life and also adventure, study, travel and education. When Mercury 'goes backwards' here you can expect to be doing some rethinking and reconsidering about one of these subjects. Perhaps it's time to take another look at the philosophies you live your life by. Are there some more things to learn? There could also be confusion in one of these areas.

Take extra care if you're travelling or studying. Travelling now could lead you on some wild and wacky adventures which weren't included in your original itinerary. Don't put valuable items in your luggage as they're more likely than usual to get lost in transit (temporarily, hopefully).

If you're studying, take care with your work because sometimes what's done under Mercury retrograde has to be done again. If you're editing written work, reviewing a course or retaking a self-improvement course, you've chosen the ideal moment for it. If you're wondering whether or not to throw yourself headlong into a Big Life Adventure, let the cycle unfold without making any major decisions – unless you're turned on by uncertainty and possible changes of plan!

In a nutshell

The 9th House governs travel, study and the great cosmic quest to understand life. This is the 'adventure zone' in your chart – where you go off on quests to discover the world and the cosmos. It's also the 'study zone' and where people see the proverbial 'bigger picture'. When Mercury retrogrades here, it's likely time to rethink at least some of this.

Five things to do

◗   Resit exams or take up a course of study abandoned earlier.

◗   Republish your work.

◗   Revisit a place.

◗   Set your mind on the big questions of life.

◗   Revisit a legal problem.

The upside

This is a great time to revise any written work and to explore books that make you think differently about the world. If you want to get published yourself, allocate some time to edit your work if you can.

This part of your chart is also about travel and this can be a good time to go somewhere far away that you've been to before.

If you're dealing with a legal matter, it can come back up now, for further review.

Watch out for...

Although it can be fun to revisit a previous adventure spot, long-distance travel can also go wrong when Mercury is retrograde in your 9th House. You might get to your destination without too many problems and then find out your luggage hasn't joined you. Be prepared for delays, cancellations and traffic holdups.

Any legal issues you're involved in could become complicated now. The best approach is to take things carefully – one step at a time. Make sure you understand everything clearly and that everyone concerned can clearly understand what you say.

It can be harder than usual to keep the bigger picture in mind. You might need to take some time to visualize where you want to be. Perhaps your faith in yourself has been shaken. If you consider your past and your successes, you'll find it much easier to recover your optimism.

Cosmic extras

Top three affirmations: These affirmations are designed to help you make the most of Mercury retrograde in your 9th House. Choose one and repeat it all day, then choose another and repeat that, then choose the third and go with that. Repeat often.

I know that I am blessed.

Life is an adventure.

The world is my oyster.

Essential oil: Sandalwood

Goddess: Fortuna, goddess of chance

Archangel: Raguel, angel of peace

After the retrograde

Mercury going forwards again in your 9th House means life should be a little easier to follow or make sense of again (until the next retrograde period, anyway). As Mercury was retrograde in your 9th House of travel, study, adventure and life philosophies, chances are you've been feeling like your study or travel plans have been on an endless repeat cycle and going nowhere fast. Your life and plans will soon start to advance in the right direction now and, as that happens, you might even see how the delays of the past few weeks were actually to your benefit. As Mercury changes direction, there could be one last dose of Mercury madness and then you can expect study and travel plans to start to fall into place.

Mercury Retrograde in Your 10th House

This part of your chart is connected to your career and social standing. When Mercury is retrograde here you can expect to be doing some rethinking and reconsidering regarding your public face and your career and professional standing – and there could also be some confusion. Take extra care around the office (or wherever you work) and be sure that silly mistakes don't mar your performance. That's the possible downside of this cycle – little errors. The upside is that you're able to rethink your ambitions now. Are you happy with your job direction or is it time to start looking around for something new, with more benefits that suit you?

For some there are career advancement delays. Some of you'll be able to renegotiate your work terms and conditions, such as arranging to work from home on occasion. For others there will be long overdue rewards for a job well done, be they financial, a welcome pat on the back, or even a tempting job offer from elsewhere.

In a nutshell

This House covers ambitions and career – how you make your mark. Your 10th House talks about what you came into this world to achieve and how you're going to attempt to pull that off. This should show how you'll make your mark and where you'll stand in society – your status. Do you feel as if you were brought to this Earth to achieve great things? Questions about these parts of life will come up.

Five things to do

◗ Rethink your career trajectory.

◗ Reflect on what you want your life's legacy to be.

◗ Take care of old business.

◗ Reapply for a job you didn't get before, if you still want it.

◗ Revamp your public image.

The upside

This is a good time to update your resume and network in your field. It's also a great time to rethink your career path and work on redefining your reputation. Although this isn't necessarily a good time to change jobs (unless you left the last one under Mercury retrograde), you can start to plan where you want your career to go in the long term.

If you had a job offer that fell through or had your eye on a job that didn't materialize, this is the time when it can come back into view.

This cycle can cause professional mayhem but used well, it can be a time to redefine your job description and even rewrite it.

Watch out for...

There may be issues with your career at this time; for example, a promotion could be delayed, or there could be misunderstandings with your boss that are highly frustrating. It's best to be patient and take a cautious approach. Similarly, be as clear as possible if your job involves working with the public. This isn't a good time to apply for a new job.

If you're self-employed, take care with new contracts and clients. You might need to reconsider how you market yourself and the clients you want to work with.

Cosmic extras

Top three affirmations: These affirmations are designed to help you make the most of Mercury retrograde in your 10th House. Choose one and repeat it all day, then choose another and repeat that, then choose the third and go with that. Repeat often.

I am going places.

It's wonderful to be so successful.

I love seeing my plans work out.

Essential oil: Laurel

Goddess: Juno, goddess of commitment

Archangel: Azrael, angel of transition

After the retrograde

Mercury going forwards again in your 10th House means you can expect fewer career misunderstandings. As Mercury has been retrograde in your 10th House of career, the focus was your professional life. If you've been going round the houses at work, making silly mistakes, enduring upsets with colleagues or co-workers and generally wishing you could get away from it all to a place where you don't need to go to the office, that was Mercury retrograde. As this cycle ends, expect (or at least allow for) one more round of discombobulation, and then it will be easier to think straight. If you've been rethinking your career strategy over the past few weeks, it's almost time to implement your new plans.

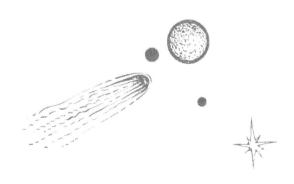

Mercury Retrograde in Your 11th House

It's time to have another think about your friends and social networks, as well as your hopes and dreams. The upside is that you're able to acquire new insights into who your friends really are. Are they a good influence? The downside is that some of your friendships will suffer unless you can stay in good humour.

Accept that some of your hopes and dreams are changing; do you just need a new approach to make them come true or is it time to reconsider their validity?

Paradoxically, the 11th House encompasses the things you do to fit in with your tribe, but also your need to stand out and proclaim your unique individuality.

One of the best ways to think of this cycle is to imagine someone hanging upside down – they see the world from another angle. This is what you can do whenever a problem crops up between now and the end of the cycle, whether it's connected to a person or to something you're trying to 'make happen'. Look at any dramas from another angle.

In a nutshell

This House is all about your friends and the social circles to which you belong. It's about the people you associate and hang out with and the people who feel like kindred spirits. It's about being part of a team and how well you can fit in to that role. It's about your peers and what kind of friend you are. This part of the chart is also about your hopes and dreams. All this is up for review under this cycle.

Five things to do

▶ Reconnect with old friends.

▶ Sort out a misunderstanding with a friend.

▶ Recapture or redefine a dream.

▶ Research networks that will help you reach your goals.

▶ Spend time alone to rediscover yourself.

The upside

You can indeed catch up with old friends at this time and you may bump into each other unexpectedly. If there's an old friend you wish you hadn't grown apart from, getting back in touch now can work well for you.

Mercury retrograde in the 11th House also helps you to discover who your real friends are. Therefore, this might be the time to get rid of any connections that no longer serve you.

Similarly, it's a good time for gaining insights into why you've joined the groups you've been involved in and what you've learned from them.

Watch out for...

Naturally, there may be misunderstandings with friends: gatherings may be postponed or cancelled, and friends may be uncommunicative or give off mixed signals. But make sure you have the right end of the stick before you stomp off in a temper. It's best not to place too much value on gossip and rumour.

It might all become too much and you'll decide to withdraw from the social scene for a while. It will do you no harm at all to recharge your batteries and take some time to discover who you are away from others.

This isn't a good time to buy a computer or other electronic devices, and you may find your mobile keeps disappearing every five minutes.

Cosmic extras

Top three affirmations: These affirmations are designed to help you make the most of Mercury retrograde in your 11th House. Repeat them often.

I am connected to all life everywhere.

I love my friends and my friends love me.

My dreams are now manifesting,
under grace in perfect ways.

Essential oil: Frankincense

Goddess: Isis, the great goddess

Archangel: Uriel, the illuminating angel

After the retrograde

Hallelujah! Mercury going forwards again means life will be less confusing. Because it's been retrograde in your 11th House of friends, it's likely impacted your social life. If you've been having hassles with your mates over the past few weeks, or it's felt like people are trying to misunderstand you, that's why. As Mercury changes direction, expect one more awkward friendship 'moment'. If and when it comes, try to stay cool because after that, life really will flow more easily.

Mercury Retrograde in Your 12th House

This is the part of your chart connected to your subconscious: the part of your mind that remains hidden and no one else sees. This is where you keep your fears and your spirituality so expect to rethink and reconsider one of these subjects. Perhaps an old fear will come back so you can deal with it this time. Or an old secret becomes current again.

There could also be confusion regarding something you don't really want to talk about. Now is the time to do what you can to release past sorrows. Where you know you have a fear that's holding you back, do all you can to see where that fear comes from and use that information to help you banish it. If you know how to meditate, now is the time to get (back) into it. You're on the verge of closing an old chapter in your life, so do what you can to tidy your mind. Consider who and what you want to leave in the past.

In a nutshell

This is a time to go inwards. The more meditation and contemplation you can do now, the better. It's a good time to bear in mind the maxim 'good thoughts create good deeds.' Keep your mind focused on good thoughts now, if you can. Try not to dwell on the past. If a secret comes to light, spending time alone will give you a chance to reflect. Once this cycle ends, Mercury's next move will be into your 1st House and you'll find it easier to express yourself.

Five things to do

◗ Reconnect with your spirituality.

◗ Start therapy or counselling.

◗ Exorcise your ghosts.

◗ Keep a record of your dreams.

◗ Meditate.

The upside of Mercury retrograde

Your spiritual life gets a boost when Mercury is retrograde in your 12th House, so make the most of it. You can expect to be more psychically aware and more sensitive to subtle vibrations around you, too. This is a good time to meditate or pray.

Your dreams and imagination may be stronger now, so take a retreat or some time out if you need it. Your dreams may provide information you need to be aware of.

If you have a fear that plagues you, it can come up at this time. This is all the better for you because you'll be able to deal with it once and for all.

Watch out for...

You might feel alone and want to do nothing but sleep. Perhaps regret and guilt will plague you. Be kind to yourself. We all make mistakes, but you'll be able to make the right decisions if you let yourself move forward.

Things you thought had finished may come back into your life. Perhaps you'd never truly let go of them and now you're being pushed to do so. It's time to achieve closure on whatever still bugs you.

Note that although this cycle can make you more sensitive, it can also throw your intuition out of whack. However, you'll know if your hunches are off because they will feel scary. You might be reading too much into situations. It's a good idea to keep an eye out for deceit in others.

Cosmic extras

Top three affirmations: These affirmations are designed to help you make the most of Mercury retrograde in your 12th House. Choose one and repeat it all day, then choose another and repeat that, then choose the third and go with that. Repeat often.

It's OK to say no.

Inner peace is my focus.

I now release my fears.

Essential oil: Lavender

Goddess: Kuan Yin, goddess of compassion

Archangel: Sandalphon, the intercessor

After the retrograde

Mercury going forwards again in this part of your chart suggests life is about to become more straightforward. As Mercury has been retrograde in your 12th House of secrets and spirituality, there's a good chance that you've experienced a mystery, or that a mystery has been uncovered. If you've been having second thoughts about someone, if you've been driven by fear lately, if you've felt confused when left alone with your thoughts, if you've been toying with the idea of being less than honest with someone – the game's up! As Mercury changes direction, expect one last blast of pandemonium – take care and think twice before you try to deceive anyone or before you give yourself too hard a time. This also marks the start of a period when you'll do well to withdraw a little and contemplate life, if that's what you feel like.

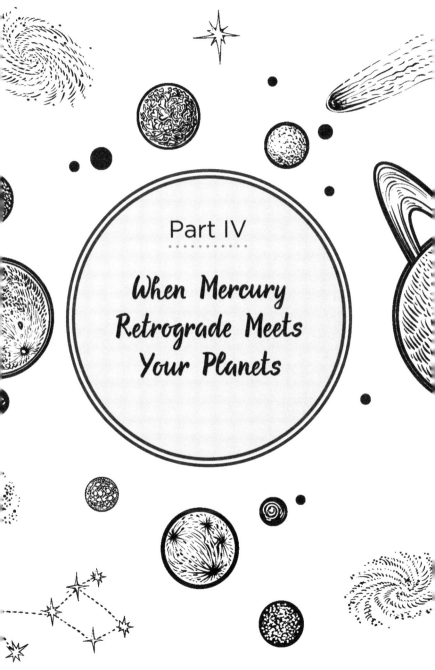

Part IV

When Mercury Retrograde Meets Your Planets

This section is for more advanced students because once you delve further into astrology, you'll learn that as Mercury retrogrades, it sometimes comes up against one or more of your planets as it 'reverses'. This is known as a transit.

When this transit is a conjunction, in other words when Mercury is on the same zodiac degree as one of your planets, you're likely to feel the retrograde cycle even more strongly.

This section is for readers who already know their astrological chart and can work out if and when a Mercury retrograde cycle will hit their planets.

The following interpretations are written from the point of view of Mercury retrograding in conjunction with one of your planets; however, they equally apply if Mercury retrograde opposes or squares (clashes with) your planets.

The Sun

This is one of the most up close and personal of the Mercury retrograde cycles, since the Sun in your chart represents the essential you, which is often referred to as 'self'. When Mercury effectively 'reverses' over your Sun, you really are being asked to slow down, think again and even review your whole life. This is a big deal because it means, to some extent, that you need to take a trip back into your past in order to make more sense of the present. It can be a time of delays, too. A sense of humour is called for, since trickster Mercury is messing with you.

Working with this transit

To get the most out of this time, adopt the view that you're being blessed with an opportunity to rethink anything and everything in your life.

The Moon

Having Mercury retrograde over (or opposite or square to) your Moon can create a rather tense time. On the one hand, it's a positive cycle because you're getting some kind of second chance in your emotional or home life, or with your mother. However, Mercury retrograde is potentially a rather confusing cycle, so to have it going on over your Moon can be rather testing. If you've been in denial about how you really feel about someone or something, this can be when you finally get to access your feelings.

Working with this transit

To get the most out of this time, go easy on yourself and allow yourself to feel the emotions that you perhaps thought you were done with.

Mercury

When Mercury retrogrades over natal Mercury, we might call it a double whammy. If Mercury retrograde is all about looking backwards, then this transit is that twofold. Mercury is the planet of the mind, so when it 'reverses' over your natal mind planet, Mercury, it's definitely time to have another think about someone or something. It could even be rather 'meta' and be asking you to think again about whatever you're thinking about – to literally rethink your thinking. Do you need another perspective? Or do you need to have (yet) another conversation about something important, to finally sort it out?

Working with this transit

To get the most out of this time, stay open-minded so that you can solve issues that might have stumped you in the past.

Venus

When Mercury goes over Venus, it can be a time of confusion in love or regarding money. There's an upside here, though – mind planet Mercury 'reversing' on your love planet Venus can definitely lead to some second chances in love, whether it's sorting things out with an old lover, or talking to your current partner about an upsetting issue. Venus also has a financial side to her, so Mercury 'reversing' over your Venus can also be the energy you need to reconsider your financial situation or mark a time when money from the past finally makes its way to you in the present. (However, it can also symbolize good old-fashioned financial confusion – if so, breathe!)

Working with this transit

To get the most out of this time, give someone you care for – or who cares for you – a second chance. Rethink a financial plan. Open your heart to someone you've been upset with.

Mars

This can be a rather fiery transit, since everything to do with Mars has a hot edge to it. Mercury is, of course, the mind planet and, when it's 'reversing' over your Mars, it can mean that an old argument rears its head again or old dramas come back for another go. However, there's an upside: talking things through (again!) might be what you need to settle a dispute and for everyone to stop bickering. Mars is the 'forwards motion' in the sky so this cycle can also be a time when it's harder to forge ahead. Patience is called for.

Working with this transit

To get the most out of this transit, use it to sort through an upset – but this time, handle it with more finesse. This is also an optimal time to get back into a sport you'd dropped in the past.

Jupiter

There's most certainly an upside to this transit, even though as we all know, Mercury retrograde is usually rather a testing time. Here's the thing: Mercury retrograde is all about second chances and trips 'back to the future'. Jupiter is the lucky planet that sees the big picture. To have Mercury 'reversing' back over Jupiter can literally translate as a lucky break that leads to a second chance. If there's a situation that didn't work out for you, and which you'd love to have made work, then Mercury 'reversing' over your Jupiter could be the second chance you've been hoping for (although of course you also need to check which House Mercury is 'reversing' in).

Working with this transit

To get the most out of this time, ask yourself if you feel lucky and, if you don't, remind yourself you have a second chance to make your own good luck.

Saturn

Frankly, the less often Saturn is triggered in your birth chart, the easier life usually is. Mercury 'reversing' over your Saturn (or even opposite it or squaring it) isn't necessarily going to be the most fun you can have. Saturn is like a sleeping pain in the neck – better not to prod it and wake it up if you can possibly avoid it. Moreover, the inference is that if Mercury is 'reversing' over your Saturn, you're getting a double dose of whatever lessons Saturn is trying to teach you. This is great if you're keen to learn all the lessons you can during this lifetime. But if all you want is a break, then this cycle can be a pest because you're being asked to face something possibly slightly unpleasant for a second and then a third time.

Working with this transit

To get the most out of this time, be rigorous with yourself and admit it if you need to work hard at something. Learn a lesson you refused to learn before.

Uranus

The upside of this transit is that you're getting a second chance to find a fantastically original solution to a problem. Mercury is the planet of the mind and Uranus is the planet with sudden turnarounds so, when Mercury 'reverses' over your Uranus, there's every chance that you'll have a flash of brilliance (which maybe you should have had earlier) or you'll find yourself being somehow 'mentally liberated' from an issue that's been bugging you. In addition, look at the House of your birth chart where Uranus is to see how this can play out. Remember that Uranus is a generational planet – as are Neptune and Pluto.

Working with this transit

To get the most out of this time, stay open to new ideas, including those brainwaves tied to a subject you thought you knew everything about already. Liberate your mind.

Neptune

Desperately seeking a second chance with your soul mate or another way to make a dream come true? Mercury is the planet of the mind, of course, and Neptune is the planet of inspiration. Mercury retrograde might have its negatives, but if you want a second chance of being uplifted, or even enlightened by someone or something, this cycle can do it. That said, Neptune can also be a deceptive critter (and a lot depends on how the planet is placed in your chart), which means this transit can also bring back a repeat of deception from the past. Fool me once, shame on you. Fool me twice...

Working with this transit

To get the most out of this time, meditate, meditate, meditate by using whichever method works for you. Working with the spiritual side of this transit will help you get the most from it.

Pluto

Mercury 'reversing' over Pluto can be an incendiary thing. Pluto is the eruptive and diabolical planet (a bit like Saturn) so it's usually left well alone. Mercury going forwards over your Pluto can be a time of deep thinking and very profound communications – and Mercury 'reversing' over Pluto can mean you're simply having another bite at this same cherry. However, because Mercury communicates and Pluto seethes and explodes, Mercury retrograde on your Pluto can open the door to some dramas – so breathe. The good news is that Mercury moves relatively fast, so this too shall pass – and hopefully quite quickly.

Working with this transit

To get the most out of this time, think deeply and then rethink deeply. Be prepared to blast some old ideas to smithereens and transform the way you think.

Ascendant

Mercury retrograde over the most personal point in your chart can have quite a big effect, even as powerful as Mercury retrograding over your Sun. (Remember the ascendant is formulated by putting together information based on your time, date and place of birth.) For some, it's a bit like when Mercury 'reverses' over their Sun: it can be a time to rethink everything. It can be a time to change the way the world sees you. It can be a time when you take a trip back to the past, all the better to understand your present. But should you go back? That's the question!

Working with this transit

To get the most out of this time, change your life somehow; be open to a big about-turn or a blast from the past that changes your life. Take second chances that are presented to you.

Descendant

The descendant is the 'line' on a chart that you can call your 'love line'. This is the gateway to your 7th House and is all about love, your partner and open enemies. Having Mercury 'reverse' over your descendant is quite a big deal (the angles of the chart are all so personal that anything triggering them is important). It can be a time of confusion with your partner or ex. Equally it can be a time when you get – or give someone – a second chance at love. If you're in love with an ex, this is when you could find yourselves back face to face – to see what happens next. Work extra hard to sort out issues with your partner under this cycle.

Working with this transit

To get the most out of this time, give someone you care about or who cares about you a second chance. Be open to reconciliation or closure with an ex.

Midheaven (Medium Coeli or MC)

When Mercury moves over your midheaven, aka your MC, cue career confusion. Mercury retrograde is of course known for being a very confusing time, so having Mercury 'reverse' over the line in your chart that's all about your professional life will usually herald confusion to do with your career. However, as with all Mercury retrograde cycles, there's a chance of having another go at something so, if you messed something up professionally in the past, this can be a time to do it again and get it right. Job offers that never came can come now. Work projects can get a second look-in.

Working with this transit

To get the most out of this time, revive an old professional aim – something career-related that you used to want to do but that was backburnered or forgotten.

IC (Imum Coeli)

Your IC is the line on your chart that focuses on home and family and where you come from. It's the most private angle in your chart. When Mercury 'reverses' here, there's very likely to be some kind of 'back to the future' trip coming up for you. You could be returning to somewhere you used to live, or be having second thoughts about where you used to live, where you live now and where you want to live. It's a time to be introspective and allow the cycle to just play out. If you've had an upset with family, this is a good time to talk things through (again) in the hope of making peace.

Working with this transit

To get the most out of this time, take a trip down memory lane, be gentle with yourself or rethink your living arrangements.

Appendix

Mercury Retrograde Dates

It's probably easiest to watch out for Mercury retrograde announcements on the Internet or in astrology columns in newspapers and magazines. If you follow me, Yasmin, on Facebook (www.facebook.com/yasminboland), I will always mention Mercury retrograde, plus the dates are listed on my site (www.yasminboland.com). However, if you'd like to check or plan in advance, for example because you want to choose a date for an event, here's a list of the Mercury retrograde dates for the 10 years ahead.

If you're studying astrology, check out the degrees that the retrogrades begin and end on and see if they line up with your planets – either clashing or clicking.

Using the charts

We've used the international standard of GMT (Greenwich Mean Time, UTC+0) and also BST (British Summer Time, UTC+1) depending on the month. To convert the time to your time zone, visit www.timeanddate.com/worldclock/converter.html and use London as the base time.

The fourth column of the chart shows you in which sign the retrograde is taking place. The following abbreviations are used:

Ar	Aries	Li	Libra
Ta	Taurus	Sc	Scorpio
Ge	Gemini	Sg	Sagittarius
Cn	Cancer	Cp	Capricorn
Le	Leo	Aq	Aquarius
Vi	Virgo	Pi	Pisces

The following abbreviations show when the retrograde starts and ends:

R	Retrograde (when the retrograde starts)	D	Direct (when the retrograde ends)

Mercury Retrograde Dates and Times

Date	Time (GMT)	Degree and Sign, and whether Retrograde (R) or Direct (D)
2019		
5 March	18:18:37	29°Pi38' R
28 March	13:58:41	16°Pi05' D
8 July	00:14:20	04°Le27' R
1 August	04:57:41	23°Cn56' D
31 October	15:41:20	27°Sc38' R
20 November	19:11:32	11°Sc35' D
2020		
17 February	00:53:53	12°Pi53' R
10 March	03:48:27	28°Aq12' D
18 June	05:58:44	14°Cn45' R
12 July	09:26:14	05°Cn29' D
14 October	02:04:51	11°Sc40' R
3 November	17:49:34	25°Li53' D
2021		
30 January	15:51:33	26°Aq29' R
21 February	00:51:51	11°Aq01' D
29 May	22:33:53	24°Ge43' R
22 June	21:59:53	16°Ge07' D
27 September	05:10:01	25°Li28' R
18 October	15:16:40	10°Li07' D

Date	Time (GMT)	Degree and Sign, and whether Retrograde (R) or Direct (D)
2022		
14 January	11:41:19	10°Aq20' R
4 February	04:12:46	24°Cp22' D
10 May	11:47:20	04°Ge51' R
3 June	08:00:06	26°Ta05' D
10 September	03:37:52	08°Li55' R
2 October	09:07:12	24°Vi11' D
29 December	09:31:38	24°Cp21' R
2023		
18 January	13:11:42	08°Cp08' D
21 April	08:34:43	15°Ta37' R
15 May	03:16:30	05°Ta50' D
23 August	19:59:16	21°Vi51' R
15 September	20:20:58	08°Vi00' D
13 December	07:08:53	08°Cp29' R
2024		
2 January	03:07:20	22°Sg10' D
1 April	22:14:16	27°Ar13' R
25 April	12:53:54	15°Ar58' D
5 August	04:55:50	04°Vi06' R
28 August	21:13:44	21°Le24' D
26 November	02:42:09	22°Sg40' R
15 December	20:56:04	06°Sg23' D

Date	Time (GMT)	Degree and Sign, and whether Retrograde (R) or Direct (D)
2025		
15 March	06:45:50	09°Ar35' R
7 April	11:07:22	26°Pi49' D
18 July	04:44:45	15°Le34' R
11 August	07:29:37	04°Le14' D
9 November	19:01:26	06°Sg51' R
29 November	17:38:10	20°Sc42' D
2026		
26 February	06:47:53	22°Pi33' R
20 March	19:32:33	08°Pi29' D
29 June	17:35:38	26°Cn15' R
23 July	22:57:34	16°Cn18' D
24 October	07:12:25	20°Sc58' R
13 November	15:53:34	05°Sc02' D
2027		
9 February	17:35:47	05°Pi58' R
3 March	12:31:43	20°Aq55' D
10 June	18:14:55	06°Cn21' R
4 July	19:39:03	27°Ge28' D
7 October	14:36:44	04°Sc55' R
28 October	14:10:19	19°Li18' D

Date	Time (GMT)	Degree and Sign, and whether Retrograde (R) or Direct (D)
2028		
24 January	11:02:06	19°Aq41' R
14 February	12:37:27	03°Aq59' D
21 May	08:42:39	16°Ge18' R
14 June	06:05:38	07°Ge45' D
19 September	16:33:28	18°Li35' R
11 October	10:27:10	03°Li28' D
2029		
7 January	07:56:11	03°Aq38' R
27 January	18:39:51	17°Cp32' D
1 May	23:05:08	26°Ta40' R
25 May	19:20:26	17°Ta33' D
2 September	12:17:41	01°Li49' R
25 September	02:01:26	17°Vi26' D
22 December	05:50:13	17°Cp42' R
2030		
11 January	05:45:06	01°Cp26' D
13 April	02:33:02	07°Ta47' R
6 May	20:14:27	27°Ar26' D
16 August	01:19:47	14°Vi29' R
8 September	09:27:12	01°Vi06' D
6 December	02:47:00	01°Cp51' R
25 December	21:13:59	15°Sg33' D

Acknowledgements

Many thanks to the mysterious 'Vee' for her help in editing this manuscript, and hopefully avoiding too many of the potential Mercury retrograde mix-ups!

Thanks also to Amy Kiberd for recognizing the potential in the initial e-book; Michelle Pilley for giving the green light; Elaine O'Neill for helping birth the baby; Leanne Siu Anastasi for the beautiful cover; Julie Oughton for her as-always amazing ability to (hopefully!) defy the Mercury retrograde odds and help us create this book without too many (dare we say, somewhat inevitable!) Mercury retrograde slip-ups!

Sincere thanks to Hay House team worldwide, including Jo Burgess, Rachel Dodson, Tom Cole, the foreign rights gang and, of course, Reid Tracy, who will all help to take this book out into the world.

Thanks also to Alex Trenoweth for her very kind and much-appreciated last-minute help with the illustrations, and to the celestial energies that inspired us to take a new look at this famous phenomenon, especially Saraswati.

ABOUT THE AUTHORS

George Fetting

Yasmin Boland began her career as a freelance journalist with a passion for writing and astrology. Owing to various cosmic turns of events, these passions turned into her profession and she's now one of the most widely read astrology writers on the planet, with columns published all over the world.

Yasmin's books include *Moonology* and *Astrology Made Easy*, and she is the creator of the *Moonology Diary* and the *Moonology Oracle Cards*.

 yasminboland.com   **@planetyasminboland**

 yasminboland   **@planetyasminboland**

Craig Sherwood

Kim Farnell is one of the longest-serving presidents of the Astrological Lodge of London. She has an MA in Cultural Astronomy and Astrology, and is the author of several books. **kimfarnell.co.uk**

HAY HOUSE

Look within

Join the conversation about latest products,
events, exclusive offers and more.

 Hay House UK

 @HayHouseUK

 @hayhouseuk

 healyourlife.com

We'd love to hear from you!